EVERY LEADER'S SMARTBOOK™

3 MINUTE LEADERSHIP TIPS THAT REALLY WORK

by tim hawkins

illustrated by faith oxley

cover design by tim van rees & luke davie

"Every Leader's SmartBook™"

ISBN: 978-1-921451-07-2

For all info:
Leaders Unlimited
PO Box 7569, Baulkham Hills Business Centre. N.S.W. 2153 Australia

Phone: (+61 2) 9629 6595
Fax: (+61 2) 9629 6595
E-mail: info@leadersunlimited.com.au
Website: www.smartbook.net.au

I want to include everyone!

I want everyone to feel that they are included in this book. This can be a little difficult with the limitations of the English language. Historically, the male pronouns "he, "his", "him", (and their derivations) have been used to include people of both genders. However, not everyone feels included these days by following this tradition. I have avoided the perfectly correct, but cumbersome alternative of always delineating "he/ she", "him/her" etc. To try and include everyone, I have opted for the grammatically incorrect, but inclusive "they", "their", "them" etc. I hope that you feel included, and that you do not cringe too much with the damage I have done to the English language!

- Tim

Published by Leaders Unlimited

Leaders Unlimited
the spirit of genuine leadership

Thank You ...

To those who have led me:

Over my life I have had many bosses, leaders, teachers, coaches and pastors who have inspired me, persevered with me and developed me. Thank you.

To my colleagues at the National Speakers' Association of Australia:

You gave me the confidence and inspiration to lift my game and to complete this book.

To the many people I have had the privilege of developing as leaders:

For the past three decades, I have had the honour of developing generations of outstanding leaders. Thank you for letting me sow into your life. I love to watch the way you are now influencing the world.

To my talented friends who worked with me on this book:

- **Faith Oxley** drew every one of the original cartoons. Isn't she brilliant?
- **Tim van Rees** and **Luke Davie** designed the cover. You guys achieved a stunning result.

To my beautiful wife Karen:

Thank you for all your support, and for your high standard of proof-reading.

To John Warren:

You taught me so much about leadership. Much of your inspiration is contained in this book.

To Graham Foster:

You taught me so much about customer service. Thank you.

To my friends in every generation who tested and refined this book:

This book is designed for leaders in every generation – from school students right through to senior citizens. A number of my friends took the time to read through my manuscript – and came back to me with all sorts of helpful suggestions. This book is so much better because of you!

So thank you to my generational testers:

The Builders:	*Rodney Dredge, Rob Cooper, Helen Cooper, Madeleine Nicholas, Noelene Beer*
The Boomers:	*Max Collison, Rob Shepherd, David Hobbs, Michael Wynn-Jones, Colin Grundy*
Generation X:	*Keith Baker, Eric Cheung, Martin Kemp, Daryl Hinton*
Generation Y & Z:	*Jacinta Ong, Ed Midgley, Nathan Gray, Andrew Carey, Steve Sellen, Andrew Nield, Jason Darwall*

I have taken great care to give due credit to the number of individuals who have impacted my life and work. After over three decades in leadership development, it is possible that I have inadvertently included material which has not been properly acknowledged. If this has happened, please contact the publisher so that this can be rectified in future editions.

Contents

Section 1 - Vision Unlimited

Section 2 - Character Unlimited

Section 3 - Results Unlimited

Section 4 - Relationships Unlimited

Section 5 - Teamwork Unlimited

SECTION 1

Vision Unlimited

How to think big and plan for action

Chapter 1

Leaders make things happen

> *"There are three types of people in the world ... people who make things happen; people who let things happen; and people who ask "What's happening?"*

There's a group of young girls sitting around in the schoolyard. *"What will we do?"* asks Mary. *"Dunno"* replies Louise. Sarah shrugs her shoulders. Eventually Emma pipes up *"Hey – let's play hula-hoop!"* **That's leadership!**

It has been a long day in the board room. All sorts of proposals have been considered. Emma finally takes centre stage. *"It's time to make a decision. Let's go with Option A."* **That's leadership!**

It's a tense Under 9 footy match. It's half-time and the other team's getting ahead. *"It's useless!"* bleats Rory. *"They're all bigger than us!"* adds Blake. The coach eventually chimes in *"You guys are going terrible. I'm ashamed of the way you're playing out there".* There is an awkward silence until little Jeremy speaks up: *"I know it's hard going - but fellas - we can do it! They're bigger than us, but we score out wide on the wings! Come on - let's get out there - all we need is one more goal!"* **That's leadership!**

Leaders are people who make things happen

There are three types of people in the world. People who make things happen; people who let things happen; and people who ask "What's happening?" **Leaders are people who make things happen.**

Whatever situation you find yourself in, you can be a leader every time you make things happen. You can show leadership at work; you can show leadership in your family; you can show leadership in an organisation or team **every time you make things happen.**

Three Steps to a Leadership Makeover

Here are three simple steps that will help you become a person who will make things happen.

1. Make a promise

Simply make a promise - and keep it. That's making things happen. That's leadership.

You can make the promise to yourself. *"I will get up at 6 o'clock tomorrow morning".* And when the alarm rings, you get straight out of bed. **Not because you HAVE to.** You get out of bed because you made a promise - you're a leader - and you want to make things happen.

Make a promise today - and keep it. It's the first step to becoming a leader.

2. Make a plan

If you want to be a leader, make a plan - and stick to it. Your plan might be to lose weight, or paint the house, or finish reading a book, or study for an hour every day. Write down your goal, then write down your plan to achieve that goal. **Every time you stick to your plan - you are making things happen - you are a leader!**

3. Make a difference

Every time you make a difference to someone else's life - every time you do a favour that is unexpected - every time you surprise someone with a gift - every time you put in that extra effort for someone else - **that's making things happen - that's leadership.**

And when you start making a difference to someone else's life - **then you earn the right to be listened to - you earn the right to be a leader!**

This world doesn't need more people who simply have a badge which says "leader". We need people who will make things happen! You can be a leader - every moment of every day - every time you make things happen - every time you make a difference!

SmartSteps

1. What promise can you make – and keep – today?

2. What plan have you made – that you can stick to today?

3. What person can you make a difference to – today?

Chapter 2

Leaders dare to dream

Everything that has ever been invented started as an idea. Everything that has ever happened started as a dream. Here's how to dream BIG dreams - for BIG leadership!

"We go to work ...
to earn the money ...
to buy the food ...
to get the energy ...
to go to work ...
to earn the money ..."

And so it goes on. One day after another. One decision after another. No wonder it's so easy to get discouraged!

Our fast-paced 21st century life moves along so rapidly that many of us have forgotten how to dream. How to imagine. How to picture things that are not yet possible. How to conceive an idea of something which does not yet exist.

But everything that has ever been invented started as an idea. Everything that has happened started as a dream. The book that you're holding in your hand right now - the chair you're sitting on - the computer on your desk - long before they were ever invented, they existed as a dream in someone's mind!

How can you identify **your** dream and bring it to reality?

1. Conceive your dream

Every single person has at least one dream in them. What's yours? What is it that you're passionate about? What's the one thing that you long to see happen? What's the one cause that you would live or die for? At the end of your life, what's the one thing that you'd love to be remembered for?

C'mon - it's okay to dream! Take the time and imagine what's possible! I love what **George Bernard Shaw** said:

> *"Some men see things as they are and say 'Why?'*
> *I dream things that never were and say 'Why not?'"*

I read a story about the opening of Disney World in Florida some five years after Walt Disney's death. His widow was there to represent him. At the grand opening - with fireworks exploding in the heavens, someone leant over to Mrs. Disney and remarked *"If only Walt could have seen this!"* Mrs. Disney replied *"Oh - but he did - twenty years ago!"*

2. Believe your dream

If you've got a dream - you've got to believe in it. You've got to stick to your guns! You've got to see it through right to the end.

There are so many negative people who will try to tear you away from your dream. All types of people who'll tell you that **you're** no good, your **idea** is no good, it'll **never** work, so you may as well **give up**!

Don't listen to them! Don't be dragged down by the people who say *"It'll never happen!"*. Everything that exists today is here because someone believed it **could** happen! Are you prepared to believe in your dream **even if no-one else does?**

3. Achieve your dream

Once you **conceive** your dream and then **believe** your dream you can go on to **achieve** your dream. At some stage your dream needs to have a plan. At some stage your dream needs to have a strategy. And when you put a plan and a strategy in place - then you can bring your dream to reality!

SmartSteps

1. What is a dream you have – something BIG that you'd really like to achieve? Don't worry about whether it seems possible – think big – dream big! What would you love to see happen?

2. What is **one** step you can take today to help move you closer to your dream?

Chapter 3

Leadership or management?

> *Leadership and management both really matter. But if you're managing well, but not leading strongly, the world just might leave you behind!*

Leadership and management - what's the big difference?

- **Management** means doing everything that is needed to ensure you achieve your goals.
- **Leadership** means making sure you have the right goals and that the whole team is committed to them.

- **Management** means ensuring that your team is functioning efficiently.
- **Leadership** means heading your team in the right direction.

- **Management** helps your team come out on top every day.
- **Leadership** makes sure that your team will still be on top in five years time.

- **Leadership** is conveying the dream.
- **Management** is harnessing the resources to realise the dream.

Both are important. But the biggest trap for any leader is this: that you are so consumed by what your business needs from you as a **manager**, that you never get to doing what it needs from you as a **leader**. Wouldn't it be crazy to spend all your time in the engine room making sure your ship is operating well, but never spend any time at the controls making sure that your ship is heading safely in the right direction?

1. A lesson from the watchmakers

The Swiss have been the renowned watchmakers for centuries. Nobody doubts their superiority. But somewhere in the 1960's and 1970's, no-one was keeping an eye on where the world was heading. Whilst the Swiss were concentrating on perfecting their traditional method of time-keeping, they didn't notice that the digital age was creeping up. The whole concept of time-keeping was about to undergo its most radical revolution in centuries. The digital watch was born! No moving parts. No winding mechanism. Incredibly accurate. Cheap to manufacture. Cheap to replace.

But it wasn't the time-keeping experts in Switzerland who brought about this radical change. It was the electronics experts in Asia. Within one short decade, the Swiss lost their time-keeping pre-eminence, and have never recovered.

Too much management, and not enough leadership.

2. A lesson from home computers

Do you know about the early home-computers from the 1980's? The established operating system was MS-DOS. No mouse. No graphic interface. A series of typed commands where the syntax had to be **perfect** before the computer would do anything! Most of my friends who bought these early machines used to do a one-night-a-week computer course for 10 weeks to learn how to use MS-DOS. Here was the philosophy - you had to teach humans to work like computers do.

Very quietly, over at Apple, there was a revolution. A leader called Steve Jobs asked this question: *"What about teaching computers to work like humans do?"* The Graphic User Interface (GUI) was born. A computer screen that looked like a desk. Files that looked like files. A trash can that looked like a trash can. And a mouse to drag everything around.

The MS-DOS world was caught flat-footed. Too much management, and not enough leadership.

Yes - manage your business well - but take the time to ask the **leadership** questions:

- Are we going in the right direction?
- What trends are changing in the world?
- How are our customers changing?
- How are our markets changing?
- What do we need to do differently to remain ahead of the pack in the coming years?
- Where do we want to be in five years time?

Leadership always takes people on a journey. **Good** leadership always makes sure that you're heading on the right path!

SmartSteps

1. Think about the team that you lead. What is an example where you're "stuck in the engine room" – being kept busy making things happen – so that you're not able to achieve big things as a leader?

2. What is one decision you can make today that will help make you a **leader** as well as a **manager**?

Chapter 4

How to get your purpose right

> *Long before you work out your strategy - or your mission - you need to work out your purpose. Ask this - "Why am I here in the first place?"*

1. Purpose surpasses Mission

One of the keys that differentiates excellent leadership from average leadership is understanding the concept of *purpose. Purpose* is different from *mission,* and certainly different from *strategy or goals!*

- Vision answers the **"Where"** question:
  "Where do we want to be in 5 years time?"
- Mission answers the **"What"** question:
  "What are we meant to achieve?"
- Strategy answers the **"How"** question:
  "How can we best achieve our mission?"
- Goals answer the **"When"** question:
  "What specific tasks need to be completed by what specific dates so that we achieve our strategy?"
- Purpose answers the **"Why"** question that needs to be asked way before the other questions are considered:
  "Why do we exist in the first place?"

So often in leadership, the *purpose* question is left out altogether. But it can make a huge difference to your leadership - and a huge difference to your results!

For many seasons I have coached a football team. If you ask any of the players what our *mission* is, they will tell you: *"To win the premiership!"* And they are right! That indeed is our mission! Everything we do in a season is working towards that result.

But that's not the reason why any of the players signed on for the season! They didn't sit at home thinking *"I'd like to win something. What can I win? I know - I'll play football - then we can win the premiership!"* No!! They signed up for the season because they enjoy playing football. They signed up because their friends were in our team. They joined us because they wanted to have fun. All these reasons suggest that there is a *purpose* to our team which is far and beyond winning the premiership.

Why does our football team exist? We don't merely exist to win the premiership. (Which would mean we had *failed* if we finished anywhere except first!). Our purpose extends way beyond our mission. Our purpose is reflected in our slogan which sits under our team name on our website - *"Great friends - playing great football - in a great team".*

2. Your personal purpose

You have an over-arching purpose to your life which extends far beyond various missions you will undertake at different times. Ask this question: *"Why do I exist in the first place?"* The failure to answer this question results in so much depression, so much anguish, and so much under-achievement.

When Steve Jobs - CEO at Apple - described his vision to *"make a dent in the universe"* - he was describing his *purpose* - rather than a particular *mission* (e.g. to design the iPhone). A friend of mine suggests that his lifelong purpose is *"to encourage everyone I meet".* Another friend of mine - with a genuine faith - describes his purpose as *"to bring glory to God in everything I do".*

Can you work out your personal purpose? What is it that you are able to contribute to this world? How can you make a difference? Once you have worked this out, there is no limit to the leadership that you can achieve!

3. Your leadership purpose

Once you have worked out your personal purpose, you can then answer this question: *"Why am I in this particular leadership position?"* This is similar to our football team working out our purpose. *"Why does my company exist?" "Why does my organisation exist?"*

If you can work out your **overall purpose**, then this will be the grid that defines and controls all the various missions you will take on at various stages. Your projects, your achievements, your values, your relationships - they will all line up with the purpose that has already been firmly established.

Then you can become a person of integrity. **Then** you can become a great leader! **Then** you can achieve great results!

5 Steps of Achievement

Step	Answers this question:	
Purpose	Why?	Why are we here in the first place?
Vision	Where?	Where do we want to be in 5 years time?
Mission	What?	What are we meant to achieve?
Strategy	How?	How can we best achieve our mission?
Goals	When?	What tasks need to be completed by what people by what date?

SmartSteps

1. Can you jot down an over-arching purpose for your life – that will control and support everything else you do?
2. Think about the relationships you are in – can you work out an overall purpose for each of them?
3. Now think of the team that you lead. What is the overall purpose for that team? What is your overall purpose as their leader?

Chapter 5

How to get your mission right

If you want to know whether you're succeeding, you need to be able to answer this question: "What are we meant to achieve?"

"What are we meant to achieve?" You'd be surprised how often this question is simply **never asked!** People can charge off at full pace, striving to achieve all sorts of things, and yet sometimes, no-one ever stops to check: *"So what is it that we're meant to achieve?"* That's why understanding your mission really matters - otherwise you will waste time achieving things that really don't matter!

Gary was about to enter his final year of high school. He was a real leader in the making. *"I've been appointed school captain!"* he shouted excitedly. *"Fantastic!"* I replied. *"What are you meant to achieve as school captain?"* He looked at me blankly. He had no idea. He did not know his mission. The **"what"** question had never been asked - *"What am I meant to achieve in this leadership position?"*

If your leadership involves your going to lots of meetings, check out the next meeting you go to. Does everyone there understand what they're meant to achieve during that meeting? My reflection would be - at many meetings I've attended, no-one is really sure of the exact reason why they're meeting! Which means you get to the end of the meeting, and no-one really knows what they've achieved - or indeed, if they've achieved anything!

Are you starting to understand why working out your *mission* is so important?

1. Mission tells you what to achieve

If you can work out your mission, you will know what you're meant to achieve. Knowing this one thing will automatically double your productivity. If you're not sure what you're meant to achieve, then no matter how fast and hard you work, you will never know whether you're heading in the right direction.

2. Mission keeps you focussed

There will always be interesting detours on any journey that you take. Understanding your mission will save you from being totally distracted by these detours and ending up at the wrong place! Having a clear picture of your mission will help you decide which detours are worth exploring, and which ones are better left alone.

3. Mission brings unity

One of the great results of all your team heading towards a common outcome is that your team will experience genuine teamwork. When people don't have a common mission, teamwork disintegrates.

4. Mission helps everyone achieve far more

If you know what you're meant to achieve, you will achieve far more. If you don't - you won't!

5. Mission brings satisfaction

When everyone on your team is agreed on a common mission, then they gain far more satisfaction as you all work towards your final outcome. Not knowing where you're heading can be one of the most de-motivating factors in any team.

6. Mission measures success

When you get to the end of the meeting (or the end of the project - or the end of the year!), how do you know if you've done well? How do you know if you're truly successful? If you have your mission firmly worked out before you start the journey, then at the end, you will be able to measure whether you've achieved it!

SmartSteps

1. What are you working on now where do you need to go back and work out your mission **first?**

2. Think of the team that you lead. Can you write down the mission for that team?

3. If we asked your team members the same question – would they be as clear as you about what they're meant to achieve?

Chapter 6

How to get your strategy right

You know why you're here; you know what you're meant to achieve. Now you can work out "How do I get there?"

Turning mission into strategy is where many leaders come unstuck. Unless you can figure out **how** to work your way towards your outcome, then your ultimate vision will remain as an unreached dream.

1. The three key questions

For any journey that you undertake, there are three key questions that you must always ask:

- Where are we now?
- Where do we want to go?
- How can we best get there?

The answer to question 3 is the key to developing your strategies.

Here's another way to look at strategy: For us to accomplish this task *(mission),* what are the key components that we must get right *(strategy)*? That is, you take your overall objective, and break it down into its key component parts.

2. Your overall strategies

Remember that football team that I mentioned in *Chapter 4*? The one that had *winning the premiership* as its mission? When we asked the *strategy* question, here is what we came up with.

- Develop our skill so that we can play the game better.
- Develop our fitness so we finish our games as strongly as we start.
- Develop our teamwork so that we trust each other more.
- Develop our commitment so that we give it our all for the sake of the team.

We knew we had to accomplish each of these four strategies if we wanted to achieve our mission for the season.

3. Your next layer of strategies

But strategy doesn't stop there. For each of these four key elements, we had to work out **further** strategies to help us achieve **each one of them.**

Take Strategy Number 1 - "Develop our skill so that we can play the game better". We broke this down into five key areas:

- Get the ball.
- Keep the ball.
- Advance the ball.
- Set-up the ball.
- Strike the ball.

In whatever area that you lead, can you work out your strategy on every level – like this?

4. The implications for leadership

Being able to turn mission into strategy is one of the hallmarks of a good leader. If all your great ideas merely end up as vague notions and dreams, nothing will ever be accomplished, and your team will be dis-spirited. But if you and your team are able to develop strategies to achieve your mission, then you will have a step-by-step proposal that will take your whole team to the destination that awaits you.

If you can do this - you are a strategist - and you are well on your way to becoming an effective leader!

SmartSteps

1. Think of a current project that you are working on - or one that lies a little into the future. Can you work out a series of steps that will help you achieve the result you're after? Go on – write them down!

2. Is there anything in your current strategy that is **not** working? What can you do to change it?

Chapter 7

How to get your goals right

You've done your master plan. You know where you're going - you know how to get there. It's time to answer the "when" question - with specific goals!

Let's just quickly check where we're up to:

- **Purpose** answers the **"Why"** question that needs to be asked way before the other questions are considered:
  "Why do we exist in the first place?"
- **Vision** answers the **"Where"** question:
  "Where do we want to be in 5 years time?"
- **Mission** answers the **"What"** question:
  "What are we meant to achieve?"
- **Strategy** answers the **"How"** question:
  "How can we best achieve our mission?"
- **Goals** answer the **"When"** question:
  "What specific tasks need to be completed by what specific dates so that we achieve our strategy?"

There is a big difference between strategy and goals. Strategies are still over-arching - they are a general way to achieve your outcome. Strategies could even be simply philosophical - that is - we can all **agree** to them without ever actually **doing** them!

With goals we get **very specific.** Remember, goals answer the **when** question. They are always specific - they always have a date attached to them. Goals can be referred to as "dreams with a deadline!"

The best way I ever learned to get my goals right was to make them **SMART** [1] goals.

Specific
Measurable
Achievable
Reviewable
Time-tabled

1. Specific

For action to happen, your goals must be specific. You can have a mission or a strategy to "increase our sales" (general), but your goal has to be **very specific.** E.g. - "Distribute a high quality sales pamphlet to every letterbox in the area".

2. Measurable

Your goals must have **quantities** in them. You must be able to **measure** them against something. E.g. "Distribute a high quality 8 page sales pamphlet to all 10,000 letterboxes in the 5 surrounding suburbs". Or ... rather than having "Increase our product range" as a goal (too vague), you could have "Increase our product range by 10%".

3. Achievable

Your goals should always **stretch** people - they should always inspire people to go a little beyond what they think they can achieve - but they need to be **achievable**. Your dreams, your purpose or your mission can be "sky-high" - but your goals must be achievable. If you have an unachievable goal (e.g "Distribute a sales pamphlet to all 10,000 letterboxes **tomorrow**" or "Immediately increase sales by 100%") your team will simply be disheartened by them - and dismiss them.

"Your goal should be out of reach but not out of sight." - ***Anita DeFrantz***

1 There does not appear to be only one origin of SMART goals. Indeed, I have heard many variations on what the 5 letters actually stand for! I have presented here what I found to be the most helpful arrangement of SMART.

4. Reviewable

You don't set your goals for eternity. You have to write in **how** and **when** the goals will be reviewed. It's okay to work out that a goal was set too high - or too low - and adjust it as you go. Whatever you want to achieve with your goal must be able to be reviewed - so you can tell whether you are on track.

5. Time-tabled

This is so simple - **but so often missed. YOUR GOALS MUST HAVE DATES ATTACHED!** E.g. Not "Increase product range by 10%", but "Increase product range by 10% within 2 months". Or ... "Distribute a high quality 8 page sales pamphlet to all 10,000 letterboxes in the 5 surrounding suburbs **by January 30**".

So, what are you waiting for? ***Go and set some SMART goals!***

SmartSteps

1. Think of a project that you are currently working on – or will face shortly.
2. Write down some specific goals that will help you achieve your result.
3. Now check that you goals are SMART goals! Check each one!
   a) Is it specific?
   b) Is it measurable?
   c) Is it achievable?
   d) Is it reviewable?
   e) Is it timetabled?
   (It's not really a goal if it doesn't have a date on it!)

Chapter 8

Goals for every relationship

> ***Dreams - purpose - mission - strategy - goals ... Don't just restrict this to your official role; be a leader in every area of your life!***

One of the dangers of getting carried away with dreams, purpose, mission, strategy and goals, is that we only apply it to our "business". That is, we focus on our official role - as a business leader, a youth leader, a sports leader or whatever - **and ignore the rest of our relationships!**

Being a leader is not just something you do "when you put your official badge on". Genuine leaders take leadership into **every** area of their life. This way you can keep your life balanced and be a huge encouragement to those around you!

1. Identify your key relationships

Think about the various roles that you take on in life. Here's the easiest way to do that: think about the different **key relationships** that you are in.

I tried this and came up with the following roles - or key relationships - that I am currently involved in:

- I am a husband to my wife.
- I am a father to my children.
- I am a son to my mother.
- I am a football coach to my team.
- I am a youth worker at my church.
- I lead a high-school bible study group.
- I am a professional speaker, author and publisher of leadership books.

Notice that your roles and relationships may change over time. Simply write down the ones that are meaningful to you at this moment.

2. Have a plan to grow every relationship

Then take each role - and simply work through the steps to establish goals to grow that relationship.

- ***Purpose:*** *"Why am I in this relationship?"*
- ***Vision:*** *"Where do I want this relationship to be in five years time?"*
- ***Mission:*** *"What do I want to achieve in this relationship?"*
- ***Strategy:*** *"How can I achieve this? What steps do I need to take to achieve this outcome?"*
- ***Goals:*** *"When do I need to get specific things done by to make this work?"*

This is not meant to sound overly-clinical - and I know in some of these roles *(e.g. with my wife!)* I want our relationship to be spontaneous, loving, fun and romantic. But I know that if I don't **work** on the relationship, it will run stale - it will go nowhere - and I will take it for granted.

For example, one of my *goals* for my relationship with my wife is that we *date* once a month. I know if I don't intentionally take this time out from my busy schedule, then this side of our relationship will fade away. *(And honey - if you're reading this - I'm so sorry for the times I have neglected you in this area!)*

Mind you, I would never suggest you **show** your goals to your partner! It's much more fun if they just "appear to happen!" **But if you do not work on your relationships, then they will not grow!**

So check through your key roles and relationships.

- Do they matter to me as much as my "work" role?
- Do I want to grow in each relationship?

Am I working out goals so that I will grow in each one?

SmartSteps

1. Write down the key relationships that you are in right now.

2. Select one of those relationships – pick the one that means the most to you.

3. Jot down a thought about this relationship under each of these headings:
    a) My Purpose

    b) My Vision

    c) My Mission

    d) My Strategy

    e) My Goals

SECTION 2

Character Unlimited

How to develop your inner leadership strength

Chapter 9

Inside-out leadership

As a leader, how can you bring about lasting change? Here are three principles to help you make genuine change - from the inside out!

Principle 1

What's on the inside is more important than what's on the outside.

This first principle is true of everything in the universe. Everything? Yes – everything! The way things look on the outside **does** matter, but what it's like on the inside is **far more important!**

Have you ever bought a car which is bright and shiny on the outside - everything polished - everything sparkling - but when you get it home you discover that under the bonnet the engine is falling to pieces? What's on the inside is **always** more important than what's on the outside! This principle is true about everything - and it's true about you!

So, if you want to bring about real change in your life - if you want to become a better leader - how do you do it?

Principle 2

To change your outside, work on your inside.

Or – to put it another way – growing your **character** is more important than growing your **reputation**. Your **reputation** is what other people

think you're like. Your **character** is what you're **really** like. Your **reputation** is what is seen on the **outside**. Your **character** is what is real on the **inside**.

Your character is what you are really like on the inside whether anyone knows about it or not. Other people can change your reputation, **but no-one else can change your character!** If you have a good character – an honest character – **then no-one can ever take that away from you!**

You cannot completely control your reputation. But you can absolutely control your character! You can make the decisions now that will strengthen and grow your character so that you become the person that you really want to be.

Principle 3

What's on the inside will always come out.

Now – here's the great news: If you want to change your reputation – work on your character! **Because eventually, your character will show through!**

What a person is **really** like will eventually come to the surface. Think of an incident where someone famous suddenly ended up in a scandal. Maybe it was a famous rock-star, sporting star, business leader or government official who was caught doing the wrong thing.

What caused these famous people to suddenly fall from grace? Usually it's not because they made a mistake with their job. People don't typically "blow it all" because they simply haven't sharpened their skills enough. Usually, it's their **character** that lets them down, because Principle 3 is always true - **"What's on the inside will always come out."**

Making changes

The way to bring change to any organisation or group is start by making the changes within yourself. Start to apply these three principles to yourself, **and see how this affects everyone around you!**

Reputation	**Character**
What is seen on the outside	What is true on the inside
What others think you're like	What you are really like
Can be damaged by other people	Can never be taken away by others
Outside your control	Absolutely in your control
You change your reputation by growing your character	You grow your character by doing what is right – even when no-one is watching

What's on the inside will always come out!

SmartSteps

1. Think of an area where your **reputation** and your **character** might be out of alignment. What can you do to change that?

2. What is one example where you can make a difference to your **leadership** by making a difference to your **self?**

Chapter 10

Your most important leadership tool

There are many skills available to today's leader. But what is the most important item in your leadership toolbox?

If you want to be the best leader that you can possibly be, what is it that you need to work on? What makes one leader effective and another not? Of all the leadership tools that are available to you, what is absolutely the most crucial one?

1. The importance of tools

Imagine there's a carpenter getting ready for his day's work. He doesn't just charge off to his first job and try to shape a piece of wood by beating it with his bare hands! He has a set of tools which enable him to do his job. A carpenter without his tools is a carpenter who won't be effective at his job.

2. Keep your tools in top condition

But simply owning the tools is not enough! If the carpenter's tools are blunt, rusted, old or out of shape, then they will be utterly ineffective! Every tradesperson knows that to do a first-class job, they need to keep their tools in first-class condition. Bad tools equals a bad job, regardless of how skilled the carpenter might be.

3. The tools of leadership

When a leader goes to work - what are the tools that they need to take with them? You might think of your laptop, your Blackberry, or your new Italian suit. Maybe you think of your communication skills, or your great personality.

But right now, we're not talking about those things. There are leaders all over the world who have laptops, Blackberries, Italian suits, great communication skills and scintillating personalities **Some of these are great leaders - and some of them are lousy leaders!** What is the essential difference?

4. The importance of character

The most important leadership tool that you carry with you everywhere - is your **character!** Just as a great carpenter uses their saw to do their job, a great leader uses their own character to do their job. For the carpenter, the work is sawing the wood; and the tool is the saw. For the leader, their work is leading others, and their most important tool is their character. For the carpenter, a blunt saw means a lousy job. For the leader, an under-developed character will always mean under-developed leadership.

If you knew that someone who was teaching you a leadership skill **wasn't putting that skill into practice,** then you wouldn't listen to them. If you're being instructed in how to care for customers, but you know that the person doing the instructing doesn't care for you one bit - then their leadership is lost. That's **character** - the essential ingredient that backs up all leadership skills.

5. So sharpen your character

Your character is **who you are - all the time!** So you need to sharpen your character **all the time.** Start with these:

- Do the right thing - even when no-one's looking. This could be as simple as putting your rubbish in the correct bin. Every time you do something right, you sharpen your character.
- Keep your word. Every time you follow through on something you have said - you strengthen your character.
- Go the extra mile. Do something extra for someone that you don't have to do. As you grow your character, you will also grow your leadership!

SmartSteps

1. Write down an area of your character that might have become a little "blunt".

2. What can you do today to help sharpen that aspect of your character?

3. What can you do on an ongoing basis to help prevent it getting blunt again?

Chapter 11

Underground leadership
- growing your character tree

The most important part of a leader's life is the part that no one can really see. What lies beneath the surface really counts!

What lies beneath the surface really counts!

This principle is true everywhere! It's true of icebergs, fancy houses with shaky foundations and shiny cars with worn-out engines. What lies beneath the surface really counts!

Perhaps the easiest way to see this principle in operation is to look at any tree. You might see an enormous tree growing above ground level, but you know it is kept in place by an equally large root system that lies below the surface. The size of the tree above the ground is directly proportional to how large the root system is beneath the ground. You can't have a tiny root system supporting a big tree - the whole thing would topple over in the slightest breeze!

Your leadership is like the tree that is seen above the surface. **Your character is like the root system that lies beneath the surface.** The growth of your leadership is directly proportional to the growth of your character.

1. When you're just starting

If you're just starting out, then you probably don't have a very big area of leadership. Your influence is small! That's okay - we all start somewhere! So in the short term, it doesn't matter if you don't have a well developed root system. What really matters is not what **size** you have attained, but whether you are indeed **growing**!

When you just start, you will have small but growing leadership which is built on a small but growing character.

2. When your leadership grows

As you keep developing your character and keep growing your leadership, you now have a "big tree" above the surface, which needs to be supported by a "large root system" below the surface.

3. The danger of an under-developed character

If you grow your leadership but you don't grow your character, then you become like a giant tree supported by only a small root system. Before too long, the whole thing will come crashing down!

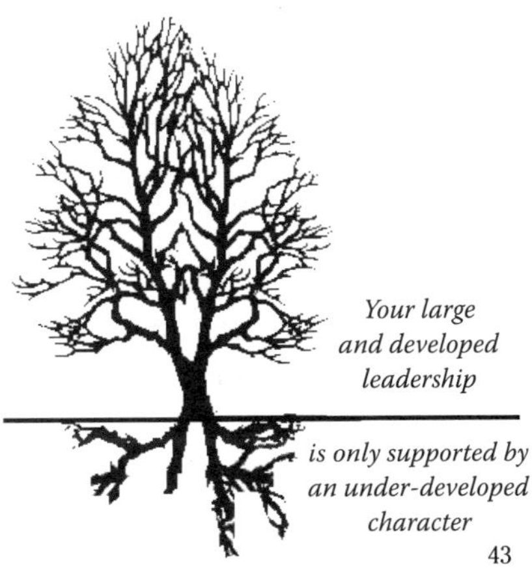

Do you want to grow your leadership? **Start by growing your character!**

> *"Most people say that it is the intellect which makes a great scientist. They are wrong; it is character." - **Albert Einstein***
>
> *"The Lord does not look at the things man looks at. Man looks at the outward appearance, but the Lord looks at the heart." (NIV)* [1] *- **The First Book of Samuel***

SmartSteps

1. How would you describe your **leadership** right now?
    a) Small at the moment
    b) Starting to grow
    c) Strengthening over many years
    d) Well developed – covering multiple areas.
    e) Starting to shrink
2. How would you describe your **character** right now?
    a) Small at the moment
    b) Starting to grow
    c) Strengthening over many years
    d) Well developed – covering multiple areas.
    e) Starting to shrink
3. Is there anywhere where your **character development** has not kept pace with your **leadership development?**
4. Are there any areas where your leadership is in danger of toppling over?

1 1 Samuel 16:7

Chapter 12

How to sharpen your character and skills

Does developing your character result in a growing leadership? Discover the vital balance between skills and character!

If growing your character is the key to growing your leadership, do you automatically grow your leadership because you grow your character?

It's not enough to have a great set of tools - you have to know how to use them! If we give a person in the street a set of top quality carpentry tools, we can't expect them to immediately produce a masterpiece of woodwork! They might have the tools but they don't have the skills.

In carpentry, tools are not enough. In leadership, character is not enough. You need skills as well. You **must** have the character - you will not have fruitful and lasting leadership without it. But you need to also sharpen your skills for effective leadership to happen. Here's the good news - **skills can be learnt!**

You learn character by repeatedly doing the right thing **even when nobody is watching!** Things like keeping your word and going out of your way to help and delight others. You learn **skills** by training and experience.

1. **Get the balance right** - Check these three tables!

Character without skills	
Result	Little achievement
Need	Training to develop skills

Did you ever have a school-teacher who was a wonderful, kind person, but couldn't control the class, and couldn't teach well? That's **character without skills!** The result? No-one achieves much, and **nobody wants to follow them!**

Did you ever have a sporting coach who knew everything about the sport - and even achieved success - but treated everyone on the team like idiots and ruled by intimidation and humiliation? That's **skills without character!** The result? Short-term achievement, but everyone ends up leaving. **Nobody wants to follow them!**

Skills without character	
Result	Short-term results, but long-term collapse
Need	Attitude adjustment to develop character

Character plus skills	
Result	Fruitful leadership - long-lasting results
Need	Increased opportunities to lead more and more!

If you are growing your character **AND** developing your skills, there is no limit to what you can achieve as a leader. What you now need are increased opportunities to lead more and more people.

2. Invest in your skills

Sign up for that training course; buy those instructional books and DVDs, attend that conference; meet with your colleagues; learn everything you can to become the best you can be.

3. Invest in your character

Take the time to do the things that will sharpen your character. Spend time with your family; reach out to others; volunteer in your community; develop your faith; give generously; do the right thing even when nobody is watching.

4. Take time to sharpen both

If a carpenter has been working away for hours sawing pieces of wood and his blade is becoming blunt, then you would not call him stupid for taking fifteen minutes out to sharpen it! In fact, you'd call him stupid for **not** sharpening the blade!

So take the time to sharpen both your skills and your character. The result will be that you grow to become the very best leader that you can be!

SmartSteps

1. Think of one **skill** you need to develop for your leadership, and one plan you can action to help you achieve that.

2. Think of one aspect of your **character** you need to develop, and one plan you can action to help you achieve that.

Chapter 13

5 qualities of a faithful leader

What sort of person do you need to be so that others know they can trust you?

Character certainly matters! Who you are will inspire more people to follow you than what you achieve. **But how do you develop it?** Here's how to develop a faithful character - one that other people can really trust.

1. You respect authority

The people whom you lead need to see that you serve respectfully under those who are in authority over you. If they see you as someone who **subverts** authority, then they will pick up this attitude and use it to subvert **your** leadership.

If you're the captain of a sporting team, you need to model what it means to respect the coach and the referee. If you're a student leader at a school, you need to model respect for teachers. If you're a business leader, you need to model respect for the company bosses - and the taxman! People will respect your leadership when they see that you are **worthy** of respect.

2. You have a principle-based character

Your team members need to know that there are principles you live by and that you will stand by them - no matter what. Principles like being fair; treating people equally; not using your power to get your own way;

not taking advantage of the powerless; being honest; treating others as you would like to be treated yourself. You could add so much to this list!

They need to know that you are consistent and they don't have to wait until you're having one of your "good days". They need to know they can approach you anytime.

When your team can see that you live your life by solid core values of integrity, then they will know they can trust you. Being trusted is a key step to being a good leader.

3. You keep growing your character

All those principles that we just discussed - they came from somewhere. Wherever they came from - keep going back there to grow them. Maybe they came from your family; maybe they came from a trusted friend or mentor; maybe they came from your own learning and reading; maybe they came from your faith. Wherever your values came from - **keep going back there to grow and sharpen them!**

4. You lead by example

When I went to school, we had a Physical Education Instructor who would send us on long runs around the streets - and he would drive behind us in his car barking out instructions through a megaphone!

Some people lead like that - shouting instructions, but never getting involved! Wise leaders lead from the front - they show by example that they are prepared to roll up their sleeves and get their hands dirty.

When I started work, I was a salesman at a large department store. During one of our big sales, we were struggling to cope with the huge flood of customers. The General Manager of the store was walking past - saw our predicament - rolled up his sleeves - jumped behind the counter - and helped us out for as long as we needed it. From that moment on - our respect for him went up astronomically!

5. You are reliable

If you say you'll do something - you do it! If you're meant to meet someone at a certain time - then you make sure you're punctual! Carrying through on your promises is a key to being a good leader.

If you can become a leader who is reliable - with a solid, trustworthy character - then there will be no limit to what you can achieve!

SmartSteps

1. Think of the current team that you lead. Can you see any of your own **positive** qualities and attitudes that are being picked up by your team members?

2. Can you see any of your own **negative** qualities and attitudes that are being picked up by your team members? What's one step you can take to change this?

Chapter 14

6 qualities of an effective leader

What sort of person do you need to be so that other people will want to follow you?

In our last chapter, we looked at the core qualities you need to have in your character so that you can grow to be a trusted and faithful leader.

But what do you need so that you will be **effective?** You can't ever be effective without first being faithful; but you **can** be faithful without being effective! So if your **faithfulness** describes "who you are on the inside" - then your **effectiveness** describes "how you get things done on the outside".

Here are some qualities that are really worth developing!

1. You are available

There's no use being a great leader if no-one can ever get to you! You need to be available - particularly to the first level of leadership that is underneath you. That means allocating time to people. Developing people is more important than achieving tasks - because as you develop more people - **lots more tasks get done!**

I had a colleague who put a poster of one of his core values on his office wall - *"Peoplework is more important than paperwork!"* This wasn't an excuse to get out of doing the paperwork! He genuinely wanted to focus on growing the people around him - and because of him - many people were inspired to achieve great things!

2. You are pro-active

I had a boss once who said to me *"My door is always open".* While this was a positive gesture, the result was – **he never came to see me in my office!** Don't wait for people in your team to take the initiative - go to them! Be pro-active in making things happen with them!

3. You are discerning

There are some issues in life that really are worth fighting for - issues that are worth dying for. And there are some issues which you can simply leave alone for a while. A wise leader is discerning. You know which issues to fight for - and you know which issues to leave for another time.

4. You are organised

Some people are *super-organised* - others are much more laid back. I don't know which end of the spectrum you identify with, but wherever it is, **a good leader has to be reasonably organised.** If you just work by yourself, you can be as last-minute as you like. But if you're leading a team, they will never have the confidence to follow you if you're not reasonably organised! Get a diary - advertise dates - stick to a plan - and if necessary, get in an outside expert who can help you get more organised!

5. You are adaptable

Don't be so super-organised that you can't change track! If the weather gets worse, if someone has a better idea, if everyone is too tired for what you have planned - then be adaptable enough to change when needed.

6. You have a sense of humour

You don't have to be a funny person but you do need to know how to have a laugh. It especially matters that you can laugh at yourself! When things go wrong, it's okay to have a good chuckle! A team that has fun together is a team that will achieve great things together. Yes, leadership is a serious business, but lighten up - don't be scared to let your guard down and have a little fun! You never know - you might just start to enjoy life more!

	High faithfulness	**Low faithfulness**
High effectiveness	A trusted person. A strong leader. Will inspire many others to great achievements.	A person who is not trusted. Short-lived leadership. You cannot sustain high effectiveness unless people trust you!
Low effectiveness	A trusted person. A weak leader. They need to sharpen their effectiveness so others can follow.	A person who is not trusted, and accomplishes little. Without a major change, you do not want this person on your team!

SmartSteps

1. Think about leaders you have known personally who have inspired you to follow them. What qualities did you admire most about them?

2. Think about the team that you currently lead, or are about to lead. What can you do that will help them to follow you and achieve their potential?

Chapter 15

The one quality that changes everything

What is the single most powerful characteristic that any leader can possess?

Integrity. You know it matters.. People look for it in their friends. People search for it in their partners. People long for it in their leaders. Without integrity, you will never gain and keep people's trust. Without integrity, you will never have a sustained, influential leadership.

But what is it? How do you get it? Integrity is not a skill that can be learned; it is certainly not a characteristic that can be faked. But it is a quality that can be developed!

1. What you see is what you get

Integrity simply means: what you see is what you get. If you meet someone of integrity, then what they present to you on the outside is an authentic reflection of what they are really like on the inside.

Integrity comes from the same word as "integrated". Everything matches. Everything lines up. What your image is like on the outside is an accurate reflection of what your heart is like on the inside.

"Dis-integrity" is the opposite. What you see **does not match** what a person is really like. There is a deception, a cover-up or a pretence. They do not have a character that is **integrating** with their life. They have a character that is **dis-integrating.**

2. The problem with image

Here's the reason that integrity is such a stumbling block for many people today - **we have over-emphasised image!**

There is nothing wrong with improving your image. Nothing wrong with looking better, sounding better and presenting better. But if I polish up my image **and do not develop my character**, then the two will get out of balance, and my integrity will be compromised.

A lot of high-profile sports-people are getting themselves into trouble. Champion performances **on** the field are being torn down by bad behaviour **off** the field. It's an integrity problem.

But so often, the way we deal with this is to "improve their image"! We call in the image consultants. We dress them in Armani suits, teach them how to hold a knife and fork, and get video footage of them visiting children in hospital. But if we improve their image without improving their essential character, we set them up for continued failure!

3. Even when no-one is watching ...

Integrity doesn't describe someone who is perfect, but it describes someone who is honest. Integrity means that you do the right thing even when no-one is watching.

Once when I was in a shop with my young daughter, the shop assistant gave me the wrong change. Instead of giving me $5 and something, she gave me $10 and something. An honest mistake. She didn't realise it. Nobody knew.

I said to the shop assistant: *"You've given me too much change!"* As she fixed it up for me she said *"Most people would have just kept it. Nobody would have known."*

Yes, but I would have known. And those young eyes that were with me watching everything would have known. If I hadn't handed that extra change back, my daughter would know that her dad - who teaches others to maintain a life of integrity - had sold out his own integrity for five lousy bucks.

Where are you tempted to compromise? Is the price of your integrity really worth it?

SmartSteps

1. Think of a random act of kindness or honesty that you could do **that no-one would know about.** Go and do it!

2. Think of a situation where you have a choice to be make. A choice between doing 'what you know is right' – and doing 'something that's not quite right'. Can you make the choice to do what is right – simply because it **is** right - even though no-one might know about your decision?

Chapter 16

How to own up when you get it wrong

> *Every one of us slips up at some stage. How we deal with it when we get "caught out" will reveal the truth about our character - and our leadership!*

There are times in my life that I sincerely regret. Times when I have done the wrong thing. Times when I have let people down. None of us is perfect - we all fail.

But how we deal with it when we are caught out will reveal the truth about our character - and the truth about our leadership! There are two very different sorts of regret – and only one of them is genuine!

1. Heartfelt Regret

Heartfelt regret means that **I'm sorry that I did the wrong thing.** I need to repair the hurt I have caused – I need to mend the relationship and change my ways. If I have genuine regret, then I **will** change the way I behave.

Let's imagine a man is caught out by his wife because he is having an affair with a woman at work. ***Heartfelt regret*** *means that he cuts off this dangerous liaison at work and re-commits himself to his wife.*

2. Skin-deep Regret

Skin-deep regret means that **I'm sorry that I got caught!** My way forward is to make sure **that I don't get caught next time!** My behaviour does not change - but I work to get smarter and cleverer at my cover-up!

*To continue the story of the man caught out by his wife because he is having an affair with a woman at work - **skin-deep regret** means that he keeps the relationship at work going but is **far more careful** to cover his tracks so that he is not caught again! There is no change in behaviour - there is no restoration of the marriage relationship - but the pretence and the cover-up continue in a more scheming fashion.*

We always have these two choices whenever we're caught out doing the wrong thing. Only one of these choices will produce genuine character. Only one of these choices will produce genuine leadership.

But here's what really matters. **Only one of these choices will result in a more satisfied and fulfilled life.** The other will lead to ongoing problems with more and more difficulties.

Just ask any high-profile person who's been caught out by the media doing the wrong thing! If this ever happens to you, how you respond to it will reveal your true character. How you respond to it will reveal what your true leadership is like.

I know I fail. We all fail. But here's the great news - no matter what we've done, **there is always a "right" step to take!** Always! Great leaders always look for that "right" way!

	Heartfelt Regret	**Skin-deep Regret**
The problem	You feel bad because you've done something wrong.	You feel bad because you got caught.
The solution	Stop doing the wrong thing.	Stop getting caught.
The change	Change your behaviour to match your values.	Don't change your behaviour. Just change how you appear.
The result	Balanced life of integrity. Strong character. Strong leadership.	Unbalanced life of dis-integrity. Weak character. Weak leadership.

SmartSteps

1. Can you think of a public figure who got caught out doing the wrong thing – and only expressed 'skin-deep' regret? What was the public's reaction? What was the long-term result?

2. Now think of a public figure who got caught out doing the wrong thing – and genuinely expressed 'heartfelt' regret? What was the public's reaction? What was the long-term result?

3. Is there a situation where you need to express heartfelt regret? Be a great leader - and go and do it!

Chapter 17

How to make a genuine apology

*When you know you've made a bad decision, how do you say the hardest word in the universe - "**Sorry**"?*

Sorry. It's such an easy word to say - but such a hard word to mean. You say *"Sorry"* when you accidentally bump into someone at the shopping mall; you say it when you've forgotten to do something; you say it when you've let a person down.

The hardest times in my life have been when I have really hurt someone because of something dumb that I did. Everyone makes bad decisions. But how do you deal with it when you know it's time to say *"Sorry"*?

1. Immediate

For an apology to have any impact at all, it needs to be offered immediately. As soon as you realise you've done the wrong thing, you offer an apology straightaway. How often have you seen a public figure - caught in some wrongdoing - and the apology only comes weeks after the event when they realise it just won't go away? Nobody is fooled by that. Take responsibility - and admit your fault straightaway.

2. Heartfelt

Have you ever heard an apology that was just a rehearsed speech? Words that were trotted out mechanically? A genuine apology needs to show genuine remorse - it needs to express heartfelt regret.

I remember watching one of the world's best football players admitting on live TV that he had taken drugs throughout his career. His head was hanging in shame. He knew his career was over. He showed genuine regret and remorse.

Contrast this with another champion footballer who was also caught in a drugs scandal. He read a prepared statement - with no sincerity - with a faint grin on the corner of his lips. No-one was fooled by that. An apology that doesn't communicate the hurt that you are feeling and the hurt that you have caused - is no apology at all.

3. Total

An apology has to be total - unqualified - unreserved. If I say I'm sorry to someone and I keep trying to explain or justify it - *"I was under a lot of pressure"* - *"You caught me on a bad day"* - *"My friends lured me into it"* - then that is not a heartfelt apology. Because every explanation you give simply communicates - *"It wasn't really my fault"*. Even if some of these extenuating circumstances are **true,** they should not be part of your apology. It will simply sound like you're trying to squirm out of it.

Let's imagine something has gone wrong between you and another person. You honestly believe that the other person is 90% at fault and you are only 10% at fault. **A genuine apology will accept responsibility for your 10% without accusing the other person for their 90%!**

Could you offer an apology like that?

4. Take responsibility

A person who is genuinely apologising will take responsibility for what they have done. Can you pick the difference between: *"I am so sorry I hurt you"* and *"I'm so sorry you were hurt"?* Only one is a genuine apology!

5. Deal with the issue

A genuine apology must deal with the issue that caused the problem. Too many high profile people simply use glib phrases like: *"I'm putting it behind me"* - *"I'm moving on".* Nothing is ever admitted - nothing is ever owned up to - nothing is ever dealt with.

A genuine leader will admit their mistakes. A genuine leader will be ready to apologise unreservedly. And when others see your authenticity - you will grow in stature as a leader whom they want to follow.

SmartSteps

1. Think of a family member or a friend to whom you need to say "sorry". Using the five steps above – go and do it!

2. Think of someone in the team that you lead to whom you need to say "sorry". Using the five steps above – go and do it!

SECTION 3

How to make things happen

Chapter 18

How to break free from the kingdom of "should"

One of the quickest ways to kill incentive and destroy leadership is to live under the oppression of "should". Discover the freedom of leaving your "shoulds" behind!

"To-do" lists are a great idea. They remind me of what I'm meant to achieve. They help me stay on track.

But I hate them! Even though they are products of my own creation, my "to-do" lists stand tall and proud as my lords and masters - pointing their finger at everything I "should" do, and accusing me when I inevitably fail!

The hardest place to be a leader is when you're trapped in the kingdom of "should". Have you been there recently? Do you still live there? See if any of these sound familiar:

> *"I really should get all this work finished before I go home."*
>
> *"I should tidy my office so I can find things easier."*
>
> *"I should watch what I eat and get to the gym more often."*
>
> *"I really should spend more time with my family."*

Life is full of shoulds! Well intentioned, no doubt. But oppressive! Demoralising! A heavy burden for anyone to carry. Let's have a quick check why the kingdom of 'should' is such a painful place to live.

1. The kingdom of 'should'

"Should" always means: *"I know this is the **right** thing to do, and I'll do it **one day!**"*

Let me give you a quick translation of that: *"I know this is the **right** thing to do, but **I'm not going to do it right now!**"*

Can you see the problem developing? "Should" always conveys the thought *"I know what I'm meant to be doing, **but I'm not doing it.**"* No wonder it sets us up for failure! Because when you say *"I should do it **one day** ..."* - you'll soon discover there is no day in the calendar that is called "one day"! "One day" never comes! So your task never gets done. Failure sets in. Guilt sets in. **In the kingdom of should, nothing ever gets done, and everyone feels guilty!**

"We really should stay in touch" means *"I should contact you, but I'm not going to".* *"We really should have you over sometime"* means *"We're never going to have you over".* **We fill our life with "shoulds" as an excuse for not actually getting anything done.**

2. The kingdom of 'choice'

Here's how to escape the kingdom of "should" and enjoy the freedom of the kingdom of "choice".

Replace every "should" in your life with either: *"I choose to ..."* or *"I choose not to ..."*

It's that simple! Turn every 'should' into a decision! *"I should get this project finished"* becomes either *"I choose to get this project finished"* or *"I choose not to get this project finished". "I should leave work early to watch my son play football"* becomes *"I choose (or don't choose) to leave work early to watch my son play football."* You make the decision **and you accept the consequences.**

Which 'shoulds' are weighing you down right now? Eliminate them! Leave behind the kingdom of **'should'**, and start living in the kingdom of **'choice'** Right now, replace all your shoulds with *"I choose to ..." or "I choose not to ..."*

Enjoying the freedom already?

SmartSteps

1. Write a list of your current "shoulds". Think of the things you should do – in your family – in your personal life – with your friends – in your career or study. Make you list as long as you like.

2. Now **re-write** each "should" with "I choose to" or "I choose not to". This may seem harsh - especially when you say "I choose not to". But learn to enjoy the freedom of being released from the burden of the "to-do" list and take responsibility for what you will or will not do.

Chapter 19

How to run meetings that people will love

Who in their right mind wants to attend a meeting? Here are some ideas to help you run meetings that people will love to be at!

Have you ever been at a meeting that you really didn't want to attend? Have you been stuck in a *board room* which felt more like a *bored-room*? Ever watched a hapless boss mumbling their way through a meeting, wondering if the whole thing was ever going to stop?

If you've ever found yourself in a meeting like that, then it makes sense that your team might also be feeling the same things about the meetings you run! How can you run effective meetings that people really look forward to?

1. Look after the people - don't just look after the results

What's the difference between having a meeting and just circulating an email for comment? **Meetings involve people** - people gathering together to achieve a common goal.

The goal of a good meeting is not just to achieve great results. The goal of a meeting has to include **building the team so that we produce great results.** This is true in every situation. The family doesn't gather at the meal table simply to be fed. The very act of sitting around the one table builds the relationships that make the family strong. If you're training a sporting team, you don't just coach skills, you also need to coach teamwork.

2. Take time to build the team

Don't underestimate the importance of taking time to build your team. If you're just starting a project, and you have a 'project team', don't assume they are a team simply because it's part of their name! Until you start building them as a team, they are just a bunch of individuals who happen to be in the same room as each other.

When it comes to regular weekly staff meetings, the time you spend on team building might need to be equal to the time you spend on decision making. The participants in the meeting aren't just there to make decisions and achieve your objectives. They are a collection of people who can achieve great things **if** you take the time to invest into them.

You don't need to have some artificial game or team-bonding exercise. Let them talk - and let them know you're listening! I love to start meetings by having everyone in the room share how things are going for them at the moment. The team leader should be the first one to share and set a tone of authenticity and personal sharing. If people only talk about how they're going "at work", then you might need to gently probe so that they realise that how they're going **in life in general** also matters.

3. Celebrate achievements

Take time to have fun. Cancel the meeting and go out for coffee together. Surprise everyone with a trip to the beach. Celebrate your life together. Celebrate the things you are achieving at work - and celebrate the high points that are happening in people's lives. Birthdays, anniversaries, promotions, whatever ... look for ways to share the fun of the people on your team.

4. Praise wholeheartedly

For every achievement - for every improvement - for every sign of forward progress - praise each individual - privately and publicly.

Make your team a place where people love to belong!

SmartSteps

1. Think of some meetings that you have to **attend.** What makes them fun? What makes them boring?

2. Think of some meetings that you **run.** List one change you will make at the next meeting to help people to really **want** to be there!

Chapter 20

How to run meetings that get things done

How do you make your meetings productive? Here are four guidelines to help your meetings be worthwhile and effective!

The cynics have a field day when it comes to meetings!

"Meetings - a great alternative to work!"

"A committee is a group which keeps minutes and wastes hours!"

And yet meetings are at the very heart of good business practice. One of the key questions to ask of any meeting is *"Do people **want** to attend?"* Here is a second equally important question: *"Is our time together **really effective?"*** Here are four important guidelines to help keep your meetings on track.

1. Only meet if you need to

Meetings are important because everyone gets to hear the same information at the same time in the same place. But there is nothing worse than having a meeting that serves no real purpose. The worst culprits here are the weekly or regular meetings. Make sure you're not just having the meeting because 'we always do'! Your employees' time is valuable . You're paying for it, so don't waste it! If there's not much on the agenda, could your team be equally well served by email information or by a '5 minute meeting'? Ask yourself this question: *"What would we lose if we didn't have our meeting today?"*

2. Short agenda? Try the '5 minute meeting'

If you seriously have 5 minutes of business to discuss, then have a 5 minute meeting! How do you achieve that? Simple! **Don't sit down!** If you have a "stand up meeting", then I can guarantee, it won't go longer than 5 minutes!

3. Long agenda? Don't go over an hour and a half

How long should a meeting be? *"Only as long as you need - no more!"* I don't think any meeting should last longer than one and a half hours. If your meetings are drifting over the two hour mark, I can guarantee that you've lost most people's interest. If you need lengthy discussion time, break your meeting up into one and a half hour segments - have a different focus for each segment - and a decent break between segments.

4. Get decisions made

Have you ever been to a meeting that has discussed an issue at length - and then the chairman says *"I think we've discussed that enough - let's move onto the next topic"*. Everyone agrees - everyone wants to move on - but sometimes we move on **without a decision actually being made!**

Here are the three questions to ask after **every** issue has been discussed:

a) What did we just decide?

Ten different people at a meeting can have ten different ideas as to what was actually decided. On every issue, summarise the decision and make sure everyone understands it.

b) Who from this meeting will action this decision?

Someone's name from those present at the meeting must be responsible for initiating action. Someone from **outside the meeting** might be appointed to implement this decision, but someone from **inside** the meeting needs to be responsible for liaising with them.

c) How do they report back to us?

The person taking the action needs to know how and when they are accountable. Then their action can be checked at the next meeting.

SmartSteps

1. At the next meeting you **attend**, check whether the "three action steps" are taken for every decision.

2. At the next meeting you **run**, make sure the "three action steps" are taken for every decision!

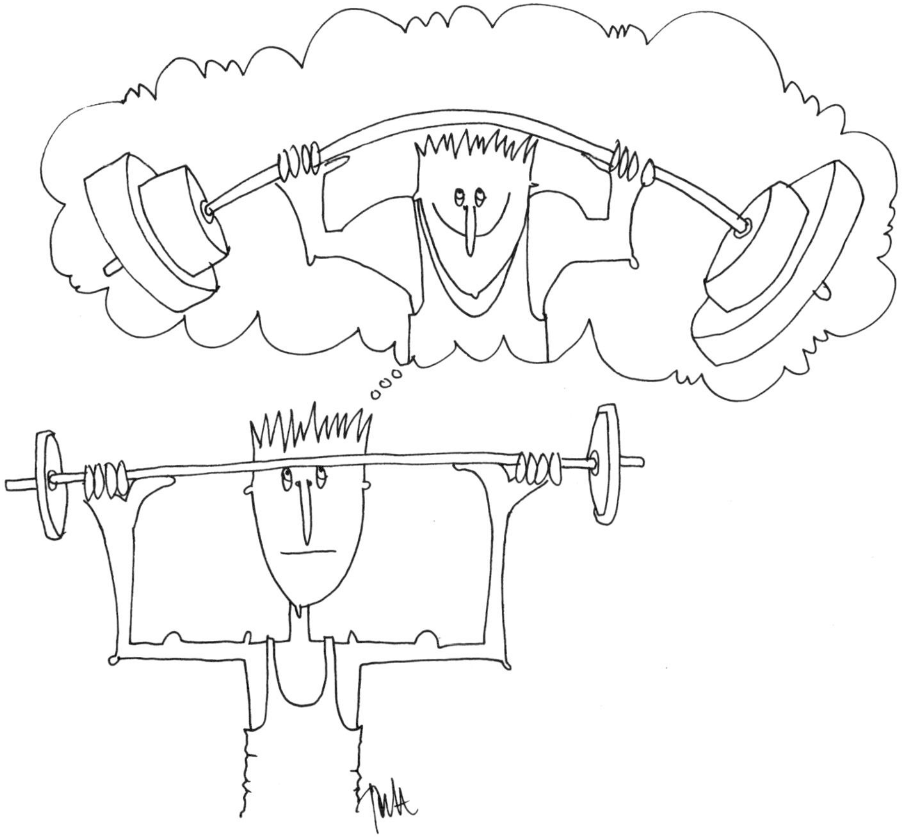

Chapter 21

When performance doesn't match expectation

What do you do when your results simply aren't matching up to what you planned?

I was coaching an Under 21's football team. We were a good team. We had agreed to work hard and go flat out to achieve the ultimate success - a Grand Final victory.

We started well with some good results, but after about six weeks we hit a slump. We lost to teams that we should have beaten. Our play became sloppy. Our teamwork was poor. We seemed sadly lacking in passion and commitment.

1. When performance is too low

I could sense the members of the team were frustrated with what was happening. Relationships were strained. I called a meeting of the entire team to sort things out. We talked about our expectations - what we had dreamed and hoped for. And we talked about our performance - and it was clear to everyone that it was falling far short.

I used the following diagram to explain what was going on:

When your performance is way below your expectations, the result is a "crash"! You feel frustrated, you perform even worse, and you get no-where!

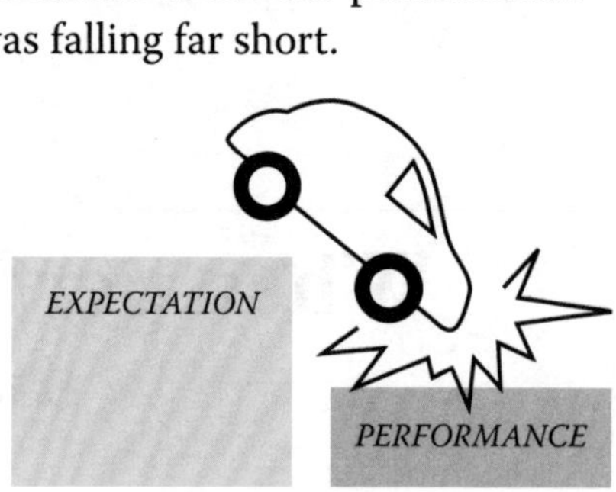

1. When performance is too low

2. When expectations are too low

One of my players chimed in: "So maybe we should set really low expectations - and then anything we achieve will seem great by comparison!"

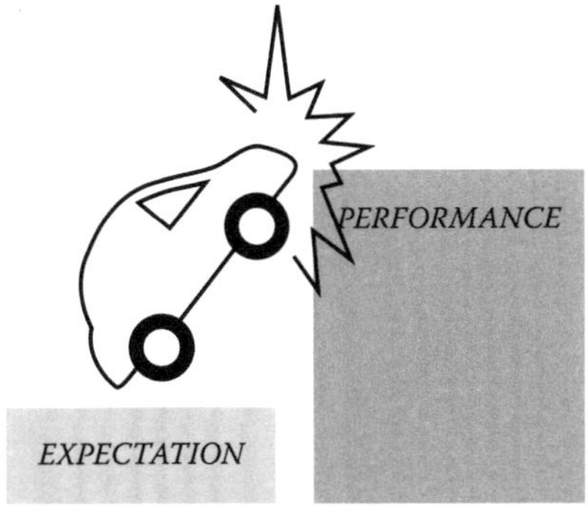

2. When expectations are too low

But that doesn't work either! When you set your expectations way too low - believing that **any** performance will seem good by comparison - you still underperform! The disparity between your expectations and your performance is too huge - it acts like a roadblock - and you still don't get anywhere!

Your performance will drop down to line up with your expectation!

3. When you line them up

The only way to avoid constant frustration is to line up your expectations and your performance.

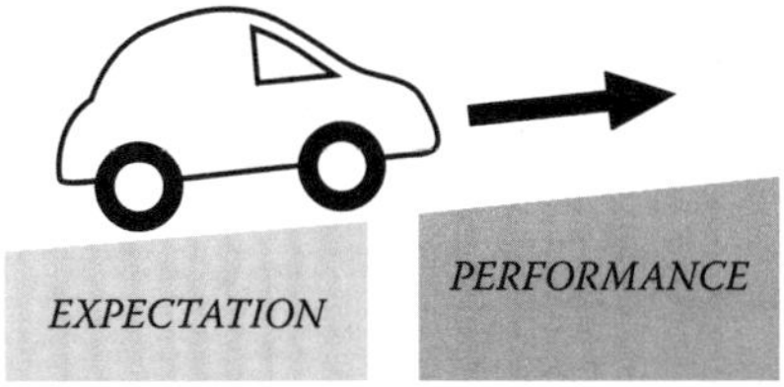

3. When you line them up

There are only two ways to achieve this:

a) Lower your expectation ... *or* ...

b) Raise your performance

I challenged my team. *"You have a choice. Either lower your expectations - give up your hopes of winning the premiership - and just become a 'kickaround team'. ... or ... raise your performance - stick with your goals - and achieve outstanding results."*

My team chose to stick with their goals and raise their performance. They started winning games again and played all the way through to the Grand Final.

SmartSteps

1. Think about where your individual or team performance is not matching your expectations. The only way to move forward is to line them up. What will you do? Will you lower your expectations? Or will you raise your performance?

2. Think about an area of your personal life where your results are not meeting your expectations. What will you do to make them line up? Write down your action plan. Will you raise your performance or lower your expectation?

3. Think about an area of your business or study life where your results are not meeting your expectations. What will you do to make them line up? Write down your action plan. Will you raise your performance or lower your expectation?

Chapter 22

Methods vs outcomes

> ***If you want your team to achieve the highest possible standards, what will you insist on - their methods - or their outcomes?***

If you're leading a team, you want to ensure that they perform well. You want to keep the standard high. You want them to achieve great things. How do you do this?

There are two basic ways forward: you can focus on either their **methods** or their **outcomes.** Depending which one you focus on, there could be a huge difference in how things turn out!

Let's check out these two systems:

System 1 - Control the methods

This system gives you the most control. Rather than dictating the **result** that you're after, you dictate the **method** that you want everyone to use. This is a quick way to bring uniformity and compliance. Everyone does things the same way. You control the process by controlling the method.

When I was at school, the timetable was run this way. That is, the school insisted on adhering to a method which would then produce varying outcomes. Every student in my Year 8 English class was taught the same syllabus *(control the method)*, and at the end of the year, when we were examined, we would be graded anywhere between "A" and "F" *(vary the outcome)*. Everyone then advanced to Year 9 English irrespective of their result.

There is nothing essentially wrong with this system. But let me show you another alternative:

System 2 - Control the outcomes

Rather than keeping the **method** rigid, you can keep the **outcome** rigid. That is - you can use a variety of methods if you like, but you must reach a certain standard before you can proceed further.

When I went for my driver's licence, the **outcomes** were fixed, not the methods. To obtain my licence, I had to demonstrate three outcomes:

- that I had good eyesight.
- that I understood the road rules.
- that I could safely drive a car on a public road.

It didn't really matter what **methods** I had used. I could have learnt for 6 months or 6 years. I could have been taught at a driving school, or taught by my grandmother. I could have obtained my licence on my first attempt - or I could have failed multiple times beforehand. The method did not matter that much. But until I could demonstrate the three outcomes above, **I would not get my licence!**

Your values control your methods

A note of warning when you focus on outcomes: the end does not always justify the means. Many have ended up in jail for using unscrupulous methods to achieve their objectives! This is where your principles, your values and your character come into play. To uphold your values as an organisation, there needs to be minimum acceptable standards for your methods.

But once you have established your minimum acceptable standards - **outcomes are always more important than methods!**

The advantages of focusing on outcomes:

- It holds your team to a high standard.
- You learn to trust your team more.
- Your team will be more motivated to achieve their goals.
- You will be more respected as a leader.

- You will develop stronger leadership amongst your team members.
- Your team will develop greater creativity.
- You and your team will achieve far more.

If you control the outcomes, you will vary the methods:
if you control the methods, you will vary the outcomes!

You **know** it's the outcomes that matter! So allow enough creativity for your team to have fun exploring different methods!

SmartSteps

1. Think of the people whom you lead. Are there any areas where you can give them more creativity by fixing the **outcome** rather than the **methods?**

2. Now list the possible **dangers** in switching the focus from methods to outcomes. What systems can you put in place to minimize these dangers?

3. Now list the advantages of switching the focus from methods to outcomes.

4. If you're game, start putting these changes into action!

Chapter 23

How to lead at the right level

How much leadership is "right"? Too little - and nothing happens. Too much - and everyone resents you! How do you get it right?

Have you ever been a member of a team where there's not enough leadership? There's no real direction. No ideas ever materialise. Everything dies on the boss' desk. Everyone gives up trying - because nothing ever happens!

Or ... ever had an over-aggressive leader? When there is **too much** leadership - where the boss "does it all" - where no-one is trusted or empowered? Guess what? The same result occurs - everyone gives up because their initiative is constantly squashed!

How do you pitch your leadership at the right level to achieve maximum results?

It all depends on what your view of leadership is. Is leadership the responsibility of the **designated leader,** or is it the responsibility of **the whole team?** Here's a way of looking at leadership that might help!

1. Re-defining Leadership

Anything which moves a group towards achieving their objective is leadership. This can come from any member of the team, no matter how small their contribution might seem. If you can accept this definition of leadership, then the role of the **designated leader** becomes:

- To recognise, encourage and help implement any contribution from any member that helps move the group towards achieving their objective.
- To train and develop team members to be able to contribute better.
- To supply the leadership that is "missing" - what the team really needs!

2. Getting it right

The leader who reads this well and pitches at the right level will only provide the leadership **that the group itself is not providing.** This is strong leadership - because it allows the team members to develop and thrive as they contribute towards the team results.

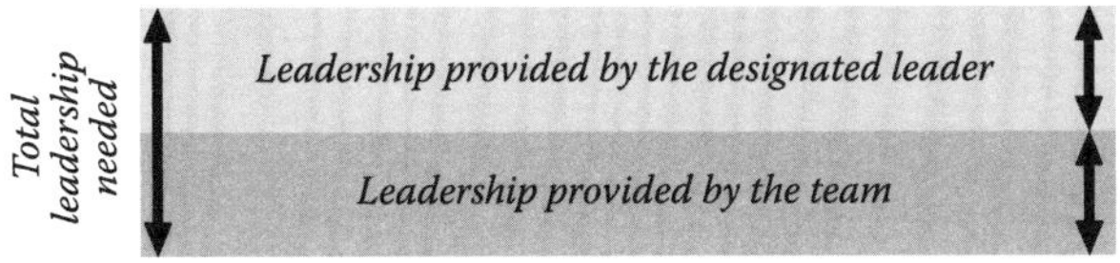

Realistically, the line between the two will constantly be changing. As the team needs more support, the designated leader does more; as the team members grows in their own leadership, the designated leader can back off accordingly.

3. Under-leading

If the designated leader does not provide **enough** leadership, they create a **leadership gap.** Everyone on the team will sense this frustration and lack of direction; team morale will be low; very little will be achieved. This is sometimes described as *laissez-faire* leadership.

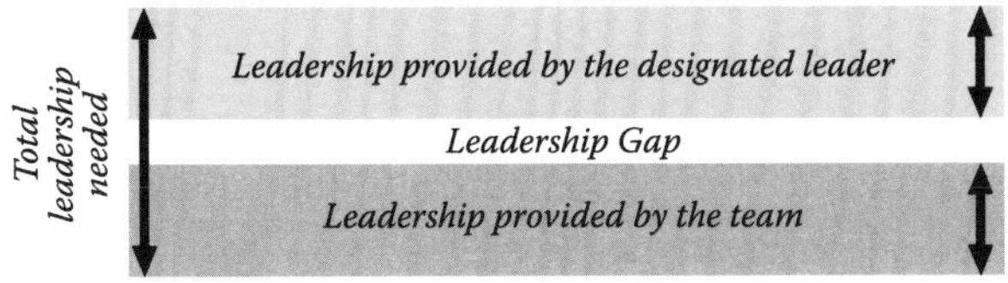

4. Over-leading

If the designated leader provides **too much** leadership, there will be huge frustration caused through **leadership overlap.** Team members will give up because they sense that their efforts are not being recognised. Team morale will be low, and they will never achieve their potential. This is sometimes described as *autocratic* leadership.

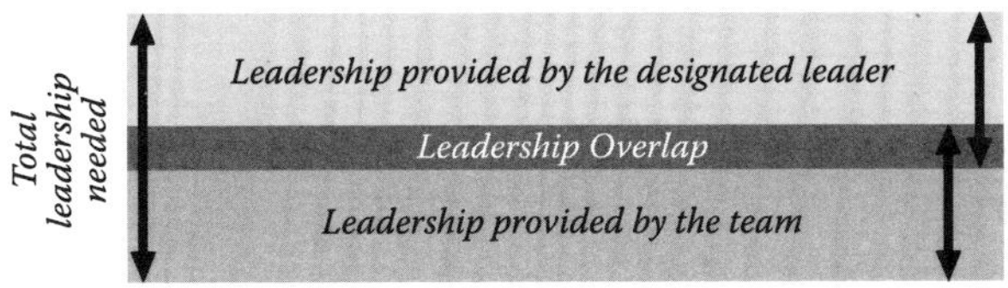

So check out the teams where you are the designated leader. Are there areas where you are **under-leading?** Are there areas where you are **over-leading?** Make the adjustment now, and watch your team start to fly!

SmartSteps

1. Think about your leadership situations. Can you identify anywhere that you might be **under-leading?** Can you identify anywhere that you are **over-leading?**

2. Write down one thing you can do immediately to re-pitch your leadership at a better level.

Chapter 24

How to lead a small group

Maybe you're chairing a meeting - or leading a small group discussion - how do you set up your small group so it really works?

The most common form of structured leading is to lead a small group. You might be chairing a meeting, teaching a small class, or perhaps you just got "elected" to lead a breakout discussion! How can you make a small group really work for you?

1. Check your aims

Before you start, double-check that you know **why** the small group is meeting. What specifically are you meant to accomplish that day? Do you need to report back at the end of your time?

2. Check your time-frame

When do you have to finish? How long do you have? No use getting everything accomplished in 15 minutes and finding you have another hour to kill! Conversely, having to stop long before you reach a conclusion is very frustrating for everyone!

3. Check your physical setup

Sit together in as small a circle as possible.

Do you need a table in the middle? If the aim of the group is to write down information, then leave the table there. But if your aim is to encourage interaction, get rid of it!

Make sure you can see everyone's faces. This not only ensures that you don't overlook anyone - it also ensures that everyone can see you!

If you have any "troublesome" people in your group, don't sit next to them. If you do, they will only be in your peripheral vision, and they may distract the group without your knowing. Sit opposite them.

A group will always be more easily distracted outdoors. Stay indoors if you can.

If you must meet outdoors ...

- Sit in the shade. People sitting in the sun easily become tired and frazzled.
- Keep people sitting up. They will "switch off" if they lie down.
- Make sure **you** face the sun so your group has their backs to it.
- Don't have them watching a distracting environment.

4. Check how you start

If needed, agree on some ground rules so that your group will work.

Work out how will you grab your group's attention with your **first** sentence?

5. Check your questions

Avoid questions that can be answered *"yes/no"*. This will kill discussion. Ask questions which start with one of the *"W"* words: who, when, where, why, what, which ...

Learn to interpret silence. It's okay if everything goes quiet for a moment. Maybe your question wasn't understood. Try rephrasing it or breaking it down into smaller questions. Silence might just mean people are thinking. Give them time.

Keep encouraging people. Even if their answer isn't exactly what you are after, praise every contribution. Avoid judging people. Saying *"That's wrong"* will limit further discussion.

Encourage group members to question each other. Ask them what they think about each other's ideas.

Don't let the group be dominated by the noisy members. Take time to find out what the quieter ones are thinking.

Don't neglect feelings. If issues are being discussed, especially if they might produce controversy or tension, ask *"How do you feel about that?"*

With the right setup, small groups can be a fantastic way to enable people to be heard - and to make their own discoveries. The other great things about small groups? **They're a great training ground for leaders!**

SmartSteps

1. Think of a situation where you lead a small group, or where you will lead one in the near future.

2. Write down three things that you can do differently that will help this group work more effectively.

Chapter 25

How to deal with complaints

Most of us don't like complaints - but if handled correctly, a complaint gives us the opportunity to achieve even more than before!

There is a large part of me that wishes that I would never get a complaint - about anything! My suspicion is that most of us feel the same! Here's the catch - if you view complaints as a **negative** thing, you will probably handle them badly. But in truth, complaints are catalysts that give you great opportunities to achieve great things - far **greater** things than if you'd never had the complaint in the first place!

Here are some reasons why complaints can be great for you!

- Complaints allow you to win back customers and team members who are faltering in their loyalty to you.
- Complaints allow you to build your relationship with the person who is complaining - so that your relationship ends up stronger than it was before the complaint.
- Complaints allow you to see your own weaknesses so that you can lift your game and achieve more.
- Complaints let you know who's unhappy. A complaint is far better than an unhappy customer or team member who stays silent and goes elsewhere!

One of the best experts on Customer Service is Graham Foster [1] - who provides an easy to remember service formula.

---

1 Graham Foster is the author of two books – "The Power of Positive Profit" (John Wiley & Sons NJ 2007) and "Where the rubber meets the road: SERVICE!" (Insight Publishing TN 2006). He is a Director of Pacific Seminars, www.pacificseminars.com

Here are the four keys to help you to be **NICE** in dealing with complaints:

Nice

Instant

Competent

Easy

1. Nice

Sometimes the person complaining is hot under the collar; sometimes they are aggressive and rude; sometimes they are unfair in their accusations; but nothing is won if you descend into a slanging match with them. It's important to maintain your dignity in how you respond. The customer might not be right, but you will not win them back with aggression. Whatever the situation, you need to be nice, polite, and respectful. It's okay to be firm, but to win the customer, you need to be nice.

If the complainer needs to blow off steam, then give them the space to do it – without responding. When they run out of steam, ask them gently "What can I help you with?"

2. Instant

If a customer or team member wants something fixed, they want it fixed **now!** You need to have systems in place that allow you to fix things instantly. Members of your team need to be empowered so that they can fix customers' problems without having to refer them to endless supervisors.

3. Competent

The key here is training. You and your team need to have the expertise to assure the customer that you know what you're doing. Don't blame someone else - especially don't blame another member of your team. Simply ensure that you and your team have sufficient training to be able to deal with anything that goes wrong.

4. Easy

The solution for the customer has to be easy. Don't give them the runaround. Don't make them fill out forms in triplicate. Don't send them to someone else. Take control of the situation and come up with a solution that makes it easy for the customer to be pleased with the outcome.

It may cost you a little to fix a problem, but how much is it worth to you to win a customer back?

SmartSteps

1. Think of a recent complaint that you had – from a team member – from a customer – even from a family member or friend.

   a) What did you do that helped the situation?

   b) What could you do better - or differently - next time?

Chapter 26

How to deal with difficult people (1)

If you're leading a group or captaining a team, how do you deal with the difficult team members?

Not every person on your team will be 100% co-operative. There will always be those who seem to make your life more difficult as a leader. It can be easy to write these people off and go home frustrated after every encounter.

I once coached a football team of young men. I held a lunch for the captain and vice-captains. I was aiming to help them sharpen their leadership. One of them blurted out: *"Well, we all know that some players on the team are really difficult to work with!"* He was obviously frustrated in his leadership. The other vice-captains rolled their eyes to mirror their annoyance at these "troublesome" people. I could tell they would really prefer if these players weren't on their team!

I pleaded with them not to write these guys off. And I would plead with you to do the same. Why?

- Some of those 'difficult' people might turn out to be your most productive workers!
- Some of those 'difficult' people may well become your best leaders in the future!

Come on - let's be honest - some of **us** were once 'difficult' people! (some of us still are!)

There are many difficult people who can show up on any team. Let's meet the first two - and see how we can work with them to produce the best - for everyone!

1. Dominating Danny

This person likes to be the boss and their views and voice are always stronger than others. They know a lot about everything and will talk the most at every meeting.

Try these tips:

- Acknowledge and support their contribution to the group.
- Let them know that you appreciate the effort they're putting in.
- Don't allow them to keep on answering everything. "Let's hear from someone else".
- Invite others to put their point of view.
- Ask specific questions of specific people (especially if they've written their answers down first).
- Don't let them express their opinion as fact. Say: "That's an interesting opinion. Can we hear some other opinions on the same issue?"
- Quietly help them to see the need to be sensitive to others.

2. Silent Sally

This person just sits there. They rarely answer. They don't cause any trouble. But they don't get involved. And they don't contribute to your team at all!

- Try and work out why they're quiet. Are they bored? Are they shy? Spend some time with them outside the group and get to know them.
- When they say something, encourage them. Silence is sometimes a sign of thinking things through deeply.
- In a meeting, get members to write answers down first. Then all this person has to do is "read their answer". This is much easier than making up an answer on the spot.
- Allow them to be quiet in the group. Not everyone has to be talking all the time! But get them involved on their own so they can contribute to the whole team!

SmartSteps

1. Can you indentify a "Dominating Danny" or "Silent Sally" on any team you belong to? What specific steps can you take to better care for these people and help the whole group achieve more?

Chapter 27

How to deal with difficult people (2)

Let's meet three more 'difficult' people who can be found on any team!

All leaders face difficult people. This may be frustrating, but it will make you a great leader! Your leadership will never be tested when you merely lead people who say "yes" all the time; but your leadership will be sharpened when you need to lead people who are making your life difficult!

Let's meet three more challenges!

3. Critical Clarence

This person disagrees with everything and puts everyone down.

- Often this is a way of attracting attention. Do not allow your team to be a place where people are put down.
- Identify where it is right to be opposed to something, and support their criticism in these instances.
- Try to steer this person to react against issues that need a strong response.
- Don't allow them to dominate.
- Try to understand their feelings, and allow the group to see that this is one person's opinion. *"Do you all agree with this? Is there another way of looking at this?"*
- Give attention and acceptance when they're not asking for it.
- Don't allow them to become *'passive resistors.'* You are better off knowing they oppose you, than having them say *"yes"* and continuing to undermine you!
- Catch up afterwards . *"You seem a little unhappy. What's on your mind?"*

4. Disruptive Diane

No matter what you do, this person always seems to disrupt your group and prevents you from achieving anything worthwhile.

- *"Disruptors"* will often seek attention by distracting the group. Try to give them attention before they ask for it.
- Distinguish between behaviour which annoys you personally and behaviour which disrupts the team. It's the behaviour that disrupts the team that you need to take action on.
- Agree on guidelines at the beginning that you all need to work together and co-operate. Remind the whole group of these rules.
- Look for their good points and encourage them.
- Catch up with them afterwards and hear them out.

If they continue to disrupt the whole group, and show no sign of being helpful when you gently correct them, you may have to decide to temporarily exclude them from the activity for the sake of the others. This can have a good effect for both the group, and the individual (who can spend some personal time with you outside the group).

5. Corey the Clown

This person makes jokes about everything, all the time.

- Encourage their sense of humour, and join in with it where you can.
- Encourage the whole group towards maturity - knowing when it's great to have a laugh, and knowing when it's time to stop.
- Give them attention when they don't ask for it.
- Ask: "What would happen if you took this seriously instead of making a joke about it?" Humour is often a way of avoiding the real issues.
- Talk with them outside the group.

Leadership is a huge privilege. You get to motivate people to help them achieve their best.

What difficult people are there on your team? What can you do to transform them into your **most productive workers?**

SmartSteps

1. Think through the teams you belong to. Can you identify any of the difficult people mentioned here?

2. What specific steps can you take to turn these difficult people into your greatest asset?

SECTION 4

Relationships Unlimited

"Nobody cares how much you know, until they know how much you care"[1]

[1] Theodore Roosevelt

Chapter 28

3 steps to being a champion encourager

Keeping your team motivated is the key to success. How can you build up those around you with genuine encouragement?

Isn't it just great when someone else encourages you? And isn't it difficult to keep going if you're feeling unappreciated and discouraged?

In my early teen years, I had tennis lessons. I wasn't the best tennis player for my age - indeed, I was somewhat of a plodder. I was at the point of giving up when my coach said to me: *"Tim - your backhand is getting so much better! Keep at it!"* Well, that was all I needed to lift my spirits! I signed up for another year! One word of encouragement can go such a long way!

The word *"encourage"* originally means *"to give courage".* The word *"courage"* comes from the same word as *"heart".* So when you encourage someone, you *strengthen their heart.* Good leaders are good encouragers. Because if you can keep your team motivated, then they will produce amazing results for you.

Here's how to do it!

Step 1 - "Just then ..."

The first step in encouraging someone is to make a simple observation about something good that they've just done. Look carefully at everyone on your team - and you'll find there's something good that you can encourage in each one.

> *"Just then, you were so good with that complaining customer."*
>
> *"You put in a great effort for the team BBQ."*

If you did nothing else except Step 1 - and did it constantly and consistently with everyone - you would see a remarkable lift in morale with everyone on your team.

But encouragement reaches a new height when you go to the next level:

Step 2 - "Right now ..."

This is where you give **your reaction** to the good thing that the person has done.

> *"Just then, you were so good with that complaining customer."* (Step 1)
> *"Right now I am so proud of how you handled it"* (Step 2)
>
> *"You put in a great effort for the team BBQ."* (Step 1)
> *"I feel so encouraged when you work like that."* (Step 2)

This is the step that **builds relationship.** By giving your personal reaction to the other person, you are drawing them into a closer relationship with you. This is inspirational stuff!

Step 3 - "One day ..."

This is where you look to the future. This is where you inspire a team member to greater heights. This is where you attempt to answer this question: ***"If this person keeps showing this positive attitude, what might they achieve?"***

> *"Just then, you were so good with that complaining customer."* (Step 1)
> *"Right now I am so proud of how you handled it"* (Step 2)
> *"If you keep that attitude up, one day you'll be running this company!"* (Step 3)

> *"You put in a great effort for the team BBQ."* (Step 1)
>
> *"I feel so encouraged when you work like that."* (Step 2)
>
> *"With that sort of effort, there's no limit to what you could achieve"* (Step 3)

Who can you encourage today? Whose heart can you strengthen? Who can you motivate to achieve their potential? A great leader is one who can inspire their team to achieve their best. With simple words of encouragement, you can become a leader of great influence.

SmartSteps

1. Think through the people who are in your personal life – your family and friends – those who really matter to you.

    a) Identify an area where you could encourage them

    b) Identify the three steps *"Just then – Right now – One day"*

    c) Go and encourage them!

2. Now repeat this whole exercise with those whom you lead.

Chapter 29

How to tackle the issue and still win the person

What do you do if someone on your team fails? If someone's done a bad job, how do you correct them without destroying them?

It's happened to all of us. Someone on our team lets us down. Someone treats a customer badly. Someone runs a programme way below the standard that we would want. Someone doesn't pull their weight on the team.

You can't ignore this. You can't allow this to be repeated. How do you correct a team member so that they will be motivated to do far better next time?

1. Keep your account in the black.

Everyone you interact with has an emotional bank account. Sometimes you will make deposits into this relationship - e.g. praising them, going out of your way for them, giving to them, allowing them freedom, spending time with them, befriending them etc. Sometimes you will make withdrawals from this relationship - e.g. letting them down, being harsh with them, being late, neglecting them, correcting them etc.

Every relationship is like that. It is a series of deposits and withdrawals. **If you constantly keep depositing into a relationship, it's okay if you make occasional withdrawals.** But if you're making withdrawals all the time - watch out!

Keep all your emotional bank accounts in the black, so that if you do need to make a withdrawal by correcting someone, their relationship with you is strong enough to bear it.

2. Tackle the issue, not the person

What you really want to confront is the **behaviour** or **attitude** of the person, not the person themselves. You want to win the person while you challenge their behaviour. Pick the difference between the following two approaches:

"I want to confront you about something you're doing" (Confront the person).

"Can we work together to sort out an issue?" (Confront the issue).

Where you place yourself physically will reflect one of these two attitudes. Will you confront the person in a head-on situation, or will you stand beside them so you can both tackle the problem together?

Figure 1: Confronting the person

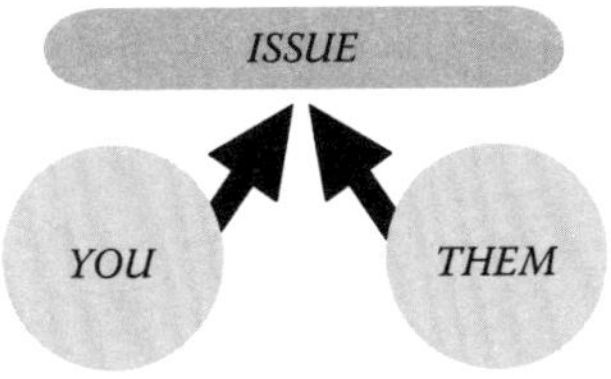

Figure 2: Confronting the issue

3. Distance your comments from the event

If a team member has given a below-standard talk to an audience, don't confront them as they walk off the stage! That is way too close to the event! Their emotions and reactions will be far too raw.

Wait a few days before you deal with the issue. You will both then be calmer, and you can look at the issue more objectively.

If you're feeling strong emotions about someone's poor performance, wait at least 24 hours until you have calmed down, so that you can give a more measured response.

"Reckless words pierce like a sword, but the tongue of the wise brings healing" (NIV) [1] - ***The Proverbs of Solomon***

1 Proverbs 12:18

SmartSteps

1. Think of a person whom you need to confront over an issue:

   a) What emotional deposits can you make into your relationship to keep it in the black?

   b) How can you confront the issue **with** them, rather than simply **confronting them?**

Chapter 30

How to correct others

Three simple questions to help others to correct themselves.

I never like confrontation. I'm not sure there's anyone who really does. But good leaders will confront the issues that need it. And if someone on your team needs to lift their game, then you need to tackle that issue with them.

The day has come. You've done all the right things. You've grown your character; you've listened carefully; you have been a constant encourager; you've managed to avoid simply attacking them.

What will you actually say when you meet with this person to confront the issue? Here are three questions to help make it all work:

1. "How do you feel it went?"

If someone on your team has done a bad job, then ask them to reflect on it. By asking them, it is entirely possible that they might self-correct. They might realise their mistake and have already thought through a solution. If this is the case, all you have to do is agree with them, and support them.

By asking this first simple question, you are empowering them, not humiliating them. You are allowing them to self-correct. This is great leadership!

But what if they don't see their mistake? Let's imagine their response is something like: *"I thought it went well. I was pleased with the result".* What do you do now?

2. If you did it again, what would you do differently?

This gives them a second chance to self-correct. Note carefully the wording!

- It doesn't say *"If you did it again, would you do anything differently?"* You can simply answer *"No"* to this question - which doesn't get you anywhere!
- The question is suggesting that there's something they could do differently. This makes it a good question. Even if someone did something really well, there is always something that they could do differently!

If the other person is saying *"I don't think I'd do anything differently",* then you will need to gently probe to help them see what you're seeing.

- Break it down into sections. If there's a particular aspect of their performance, ask about that specific detail. *"So, can I ask you how you thought your introduction went?". "Can we look at the incident when those customers were complaining?"*
- Make your own observation. *"Can I let you know something I noticed?". "Can I tell you the difficulty I saw?"*

Keep gently probing until the two of you have some agreement on where the problem was. Then you can move on to the third question:

3. How can I help you next time this comes around?

This question communicates a number of important values:

- It empowers the other person to nominate how they would like your help, rather than you imposing something on them.
- It supports the person by letting them know that you are there ready to help them.
- It trusts the other person by suggesting to them that there will be a "next time".

Your aim as a leader is to help make everyone else a winner. By being **gentle** with the person while you are **firm** with their issue, you will achieve great loyalty - and great teamwork!

SmartSteps

1. Think about a time where you had to correct someone. How did you both handle it? How did it turn out?

2. The next time you need to correct someone, work through the three key questions:

   a) *"How do you feel it went?"*

   b) *"If you did it again, what would you do differently?"*

   c) *"How can I help you next time this comes around?"*

Chapter 31

How to confront others

Sometimes there are issues that we simply must confront with people. Here's how to ensure the best possible outcome.

Sometimes there are issues which are so important - or so urgent - that you need to confront them immediately. Someone's behaviour is way out of line. Someone's attitude is verging on defiance. Something is going wrong which might have serious consequences.

You need to raise some issues with a team member that might have difficult consequences. You've worked through all the steps, but without success. How do you deal with this?

1. Don't do it alone

If you think difficult decisions have to be made, confide in a colleague whom you trust. Gain someone else's wisdom just to make sure that you're seeing things correctly.

2. Admit your vulnerability

You don't have to play the "big bad boss" card. If you need to point out to someone that you think they're wrong, it's okay to admit that **you** sometimes get things wrong. You have a much greater chance of success if your team member sees you as a fellow-struggler.

"Look, I might have got this issue wrong ..."

This will make it easier for your team member to hear what you have to say.

3. Ask for understanding

If what you are about to say will be difficult for the other person to hear, ask for their understanding.

"What I'm about to say to you is a little difficult. I even feel a bit awkward raising it with you."

4. Make an observation

Ask them if you can make an observation about a particular issue. Simply describe to them **what you have observed.** At this point, don't read any interpretation into it. Don't make any reaction to it. Simply let them know what you've observed.

5. Check your observation

Simply ask them if they think your observation was correct. That is, did it really happen that way? Sometimes there could be a simple misunderstanding. Sometimes by clarifying what actually happened, a lot of issues get resolved without further investigation.

When you have some agreement on what actually happened, then you can check your **interpretation** - that is - what did all this **mean**?

6. Make your interpretation

Here is the formula:

"When I saw X happen, I felt Y"

Here's an example:

"When I saw you yelling at that customer, I felt like you had lost control."

7. Check your interpretation

Check whether the way you're interpreting things is correct. Ask them: *"Is that what you think happened too?"*

8. Agree on the consequences

Ask *"What do you think should happen next?"* If the other person's answer is close enough, then accept it, agree to it, and implement it.

If not, then you will need to say: *"Here's what I think the next step should be".* Where possible, the "next step" is to help your team member never get into this mess again. It takes much more effort to train a new staff member than to keep an existing one, so do everything you can to work with this person to achieve a great outcome.

9. Only play the "boss" card if absolutely necessary.

Try to get agreement first. Only as a last resort do you say: *"As the team leader here, I now need to make the final decision".* If you play the "boss" card too often, you will never build a loyal staff.

SmartSteps

1. Think back to a time where you needed to confront a person about an issue. How did it go?

2. What could you do **differently** next time to produce a better outcome?

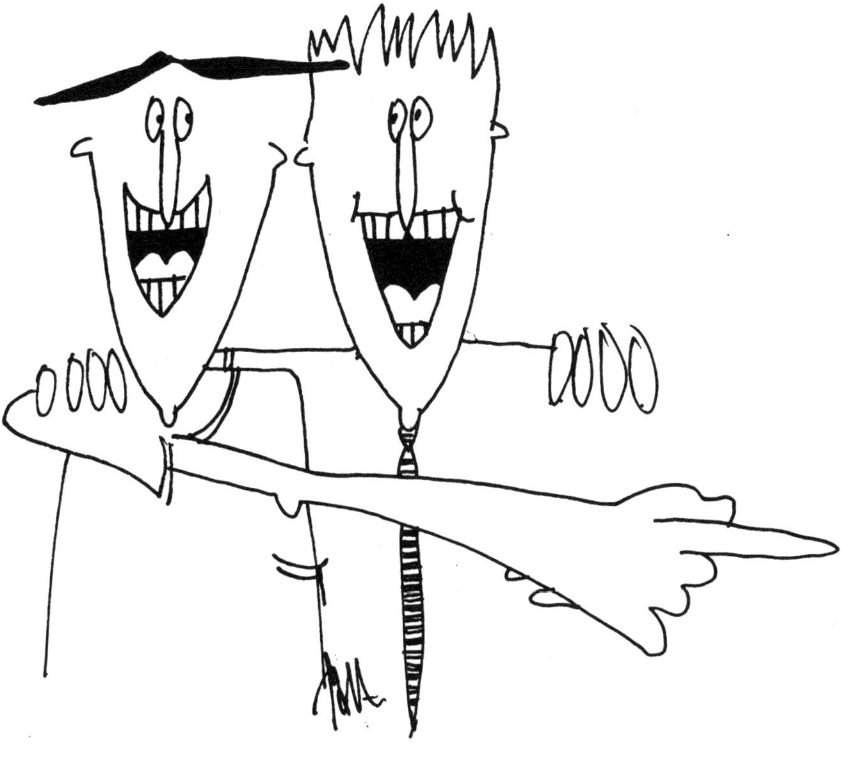

Chapter 32

The art of successful delegation

How can you help people feel needed, without making them feel used?

Can you remember the last time that someone asked you to do a job for them? Did you walk away from this experience feeling **needed** - or did you walk away feeling **used?** You know how different each of these feels. If you feel needed - then you'll come back and do this same job over and over again. But if you feel used, then you'll do everything you can to avoid feeling so belittled again.

Think about the people who help you at the moment. Are they feeling needed - or are they feeling used?

There are two ways to enlist someone else's support for a task. One is genuine delegation - the other is merely "dumping" this job on a person. What's the difference? We all know the importance of delegation. How can we do it well so that we inspire people to high levels of achievement?

1. True delegation avoids merely "dumping"

Here's how "dumping" works: you find the jobs that you hate doing, and you dump them on somebody else. You can't stand making phone calls - so you get someone else to do them. You can't be bothered with the details of organising a roster - so you get someone else to do it.

While there is great value in finding others to complement your skill set - if you discover you're only getting rid of the jobs you **hate**, there is a strong possibility that the other person will feel used!

If you want to delegate a job that you genuinely dislike - then do it **with** the other person - and show them that you're ready to roll up your sleeves!

2. True delegation focuses on partnership

What's the way to help someone feel wanted? Pick a task that you're good at - something you enjoy - and invite someone else to partner with you. *"This really matters to our organisation - can you help me with it?"* Take their ideas on board - teach them the best way - work in partnership together and slowly release them to keep going without you.

Then **you** are freed up to go and achieve new things.
That's genuine delegation!

3. True delegation focuses on support

The quickest way to make someone feel used is to give them a job, then leave them to it and never offer any support.

A man I know offered to join a 'clean-up day' at his child's sporting club. When he arrived, he was handed a tin of paint and a paintbrush, and told to paint a large wall. He worked on this all day - without anyone checking back on him - without anyone working with him - without any feedback or encouragement. At the end of the day, he finished his task, and decided **he was never going to be used like that again!**

4. True delegation focuses on appreciation

If you want someone to feel **needed** rather than **used,** then you need to keep telling them how much they are appreciated. No-one likes being taken for granted, but in so many businesses and other organisations, that's exactly how people feel.

SmartSteps

1. Think through the people who are helping you at the moment:

   a) Are there any instances where you might have **dumped** them with the job, rather than **delegating** it?

   b) What can you now do differently to help people to feel **needed** rather than feeling **used?**

Chapter 33

How to remember names Part 1

It's been described as "the sweetest sound" [1] *- that someone else cares enough to know you by name. But how do you do it?*

I have a confession to make. I am the world's worst person at remembering names! Right after the person introduces themselves *"Hi - My name is Bob!"* - roughly 10 seconds later I have the most horrible realisation - *"I've forgotten their name already!"* Has this happened to you? Relax - you're in good company! As a fellow struggler - let me share with you what I've learnt - and believe me - **I've had to learn the hard way!**

1. The other person's number one need

You must be convinced of one thing - that when you're meeting a person, the most important thing to them is **that you remember their name!** Every one of us needs to know that we matter. When you recognise and remember a person's name - you communicate to them - *"You matter to me!".* Similarly, if you **don't** remember their name, guess what you communicate? So - take the time to remember their name - **it's what they really want from you!**

2. YOUR number one priority

You must understand, that when you are meeting a person, **your** number one priority is to **listen to and remember their name.** Often

1 Dale Carnegie "How to Win Friends and Influence People" (Pocket Books/Simon and Schuster Inc. NY 1981) p.79

when I meet people, I'm thinking about the impression I will make, or what I will say to them next. Or when they're introducing themselves, I'm thinking about how I will reply. I am learning to put all those things on hold. Yes - they all matter - and yes, I will get to them eventually. But remember - when you are meeting a person - first up - you only have **one** job - **to remember their name!**

3. Use their name immediately

Just before you dazzle them with your amazing personality, **use their name straight away**! This achieves a number of things:

- It encourages the other person.
- It personalises the conversation.
- It communicates that the other person matters to you.
- The repetition of their name will help you to remember it.

It's quite easy - it doesn't have to be forced.

"Hi - My name is Bob!"

"It's great to meet you, Bob"

4. If appropriate, comment on their name.

If someone has an interesting or unusual name, I will often comment on it:

"What a fantastic name"

"That's an intriguing name"

"Nice to meet you Bob. And what's your last name?"

A simple question - asked tactfully - will help you remember their name.

5. Repeat their name appropriately

Don't overdo this one, but try to use their name a couple of times during your conversation. If nothing else, use their name again when you farewell them.

6. Write down their name as soon as possible

After you have finished your conversation, write down their name - and something about them - to help you to remember them. Use their business card if they have given it to you. Keep these names in a notebook for future reference.

For many people - this is all you need! But for those of you - who, like me - **still need extra help** - we'll learn some really fun things in the next chapter!

SmartSteps

1. Can you think of a time where you met a new person and forgot their name in the first few minutes? Or where you couldn't remember it next time you met them?

    a) The next time you meet somebody new, try the 6 steps outline above.

    b) Did the 6 steps help? How did it go?

Chapter 34

How to remember names Part 2

> *If remembering names is a nightmare for you, then try these fun memory tips that will make an amazing difference!*

I struggle to remember names. Even when I am trying hard, people's names seem to escape through a mystery vent I have in my brain somewhere. If you really struggle in this area - then try these memory tips. They may sound crazy - **but they work!**

Do not neglect the procedures outlined in the previous chapter. Use these memory aids **in conjunction** with what you've already learned.

1. Turn the other person's name into a wild picture

This might be hard at first, but the more you do it, the easier it will get. When you first hear a person's name - **turn it into a picture** - a wild picture! That is, try to imagine something outrageous that sounds like their name!

Some names are dead easy. When I meet someone called *John,* I immediately think of a *toilet.* (the naval term). When I meet someone called *Paul,* I think of someone carrying a coffin (*a pall-bearer*). If you want to remember **my** name (*Tim*), then you might think of a *Tim-Tam* (an Aussie chocolate biscuit); or you might think of a *tin* (sounds similar), or you might think of a *clock* (The clock represents *time* - which is a similar word to *Tim*).

Some names are harder. Try breaking them down into their syllables. Try altering the sound of the syllables so you can think of a picture.

A name I always struggle to find a picture for is *Nathan*. I break it down into its syllables - *"Nay"* and *"than".* *"Nay"* is like the sound a horse makes, so I start thinking of a horse. "*Than*" is harder. It might sound like "*thin*" - so I will think of a very skinny horse. Or it might sound like "*sand*" - so I think of a horse stuck in the sand.

There are no right or wrong answers. The important thing is that the picture makes the connection for you.

See if you can turn each of these names into a wild picture:

Easy	**Harder**
Shelly	Steve
Russell	Eric
Mat	Tanya
Barbie	Stacey
Mason	Lynne

2. Turn the other person's most obvious visual feature into a picture

Now for a second picture! What's the most obvious thing you notice about the other person's appearance? Is it their thick wasp of blonde hair? Is it the craggy little glasses hanging off their nose? Often the feature you notice will be their **worst** feature! (so don't tell them about it!) If you're really stuck, use something obvious that they're wearing. (It won't help you when you meet them in the future, but it will get you through your first meeting!)

You might be wondering what you are going to do with these two stupid crazy pictures. If you've met someone called Dave, who has a big bushy moustache, you might have 2 pictures in your head:

- A picture of some Tarzan guy diving off a high cliff ("Dive" = "Dave")
- A big bushy moustache

What do you do with those? All will be revealed in the next chapter! But do keep the pictures stupid and crazy! The wilder they are - the more improbable they are - the better you will be able to remember them!

Some further clues

Here are my first thoughts on the 10 names I asked you to picture. These are not the only "right" answers - they might not even be the best answers! The pictures YOU worked out are the ones that will work best for you. But if you need a little guidance, here are my first thoughts:

Shelly	Lots of shells on a beach
Russell	Leaves swirling in the wind
Mat	The front door welcome mat
Barbie	Backyard BBQ
Mason	A stone-cutter at work
Steve	A stove
Eric	A big letter 'E' pulling a rickshaw
Tanya	10 ewes lined up on a farm
Stacey	A holiday at the beach (Stay - sea!)
Lynne	A line down the centre of the road

SmartSteps

1. If you haven't done it already, try and work out your own *word pictures* for the ten names above (don't look at my suggestions!) Try and work out a crazy picture to help you recall each name.

2. The next time you meet someone new, **try it!** Try and think of a crazy word picture to remind you of their name, and try and think of another crazy word picture to describe their most obvious visual feature. Could you work out these two picture? Did it help your memory?

Chapter 35

How to remember names Part 3

How do you form a picture in your mind that will give you instant recall to anyone's name?

You are well on your way to being a champion at remembering names!

- You've taken the time to listen to and use the person's name a number of times (Chapter #33).
- You've turned their name into a crazy picture.
- You've turned their most obvious visual feature into a crazy picture.
- You now have two crazy pictures in your head (Chapter #34).

Now comes the fun!

1. Put the 2 pictures together

Take the picture of the person's name and put it together with the picture of their most obvious visual feature to form a crazy, outrageous and impossible picture!

Example A:

- Remember the man we met in Chapter 34? The man called Dave - with the big bushy moustache?
- We formed two pictures:
    - A Tarzan figure diving off a high cliff. (Dave = "Dive").
    - A big bushy moustache.
- Can you put the two pictures together?
    - A huge moustache - covered in a Tarzan loin-cloth - diving off a cliff.
    - Or perhaps a Tarzan figure diving into a river full of giant moustaches.
- **Don't** just picture Tarzan with a moustache. It's too ordinary. Too forgettable. Your picture has to be unrealistic - vivid - and full of crazy action!

Example B:

- I met a man called Luke. I turned his name into "look" - and I pictured that as a telescope.
- His most obvious visual feature was his tight curly hair.
- By putting the two pictures together, I imagined thousands of tiny telescopes - each one hanging off one of his curls - with little men looking into each telescope - and turning their telescopes to look at me (with horror on their faces)!
- Every time I see him, the moment I see his curly hair - I instantly "see" all those tiny telescopes - I instantly think of the name "Luke".

2. Your picture must be outrageous

If the picture isn't outrageous, you won't remember it. Your picture needs to be "cartoon-like" - that is - absolutely impossible and ridiculous.

If you meet someone called "Andy", there's no use just picturing him as a hand. Too mundane! Picture him as a giant hand flapping around on his head - or 1000 hands leaping out all over his body!

3. Your picture must be full of action

Your picture shouldn't be still. It needs to be animated - full of action - gross, comical, outrageous action. The wackier - the better!

4. Your picture should involve you

Wherever you can, put **yourself** in the picture. If **you're** in the picture, then you will be far more involved, and far more likely to remember what you've pictured. Notice that in my example, the telescopes in Luke's hair were pointing at **me**!

Does all this sound crazy? **Try it - it works!** It will feel awkward when you start - it will take a bit of time - but the more you practise, the faster it will come, and the better you will be at remembering **everyone's** name!

Go and practise now! Practise with everyone you meet. Train your mind to think in vivid pictures!

SmartSteps

1. The next new person you meet, work through the steps:

   a) Turn their name into a comical, crazy, wacky picture.

   b) Turn their most obvious visual point into a humorous and vivid picture.

   c) Put the two pictures together into a comical and energetic picture – with lots of action – that involves **you!**

   d) Practise on everyone you meet – the checkout operator, the store clerk, the new person at your club ... The more you practise – the better (and faster) you will get – and you're well on your way to being a champion at remembering names!

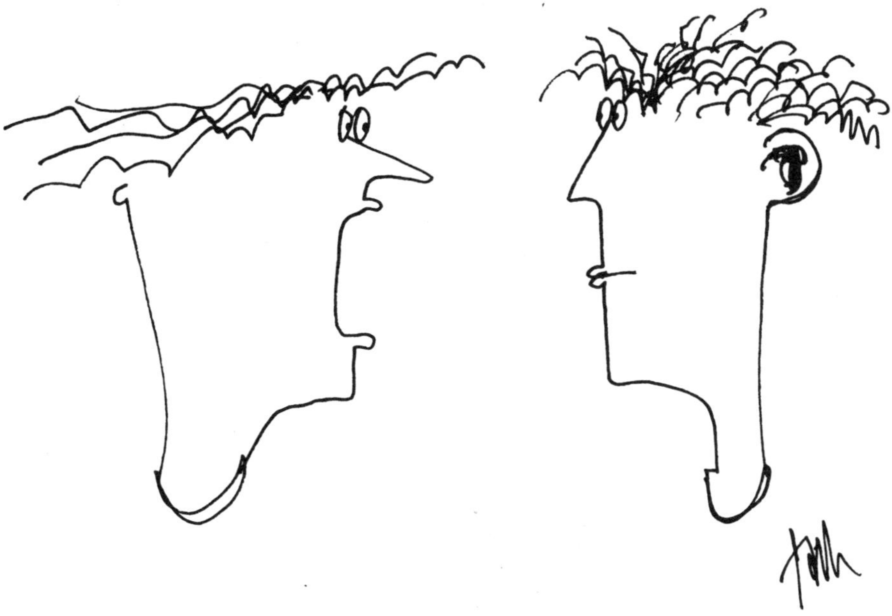

Chapter 36

8 common mistakes in listening

Most people think listening is automatic. If my ears are open, and someone else is talking, then I must be listening! Right?

Wrong! We all learn at an early age that you can be right in front of a person and not hear a word that they are saying! As children, we learned to say *"Yes, Mum!"* or *"No, Dad"* **without ever hearing a word that had been said!** How many married couples are there where one person says of their partner *"They never listen to a word I say!"*

Listening is not automatic. Listening requires hard work. Listening is a skill to be learned. It is so vital. Most people when they are talking about something that has happened in their day **simply want someone else to listen.** By learning to listen well, you can resolve conflicts, restore relationships, inspire confidence and unleash people to achieve their potential! Does that sound like something worth learning?

Before we learn the steps, let's go through the eight common mistakes in listening.

1. Dismiss them

When you don't think that what the other person is saying is very important, or you're trying to downplay the seriousness of their situation, it's easy to dismiss what they're saying.

> *"You shouldn't worry about that!"*
>
> *"I don't think that really matters"*
>
> *"That's not the important issue, is it?"*

You may well be right, but the other person thinks that what they're saying is important - otherwise they wouldn't be saying it! So don't dismiss what they say!

2. Give advice

"Here's what you should do!"

You may well be right, but most people don't say things because they want advice. They say things **because they want to be listened to.** Your advice might be helpful further down the track, but if you give advice straight out, its another way of dismissing the person. To them it can sound like:

"Here's your answer - now go away!"

3. Over-empathise

"I know exactly how you feel!"

No you don't. You know how **you** feel, and you can **imagine** how the other person feels, but believe me, **you don't know how THEY feel!**

4. Ask lots of questions

There's a time for this. But not yet. Before you ask questions you need to really listen and let the person know you've heard them.

5. Finish their sentences

When people are hesitant or slow, there is a real temptation to finish their sentences for them. Resist the urge! You might well put your **own** words into **their** mouth!

6. Take over

"You know, something just like that happened to me. Let me tell you about it!"

How will the other person feel when you completely hijack the conversation? It's another way of dismissing them!

7. Interrupt

Don't! Let them have their say! How do you feel when people interrupt you?

8. Formulate your reply

Have you ever talked to someone, and the whole time you're speaking, you know that they're thinking of their clever reply? **Take the time to listen to them!**

How do you do that? Next chapter!

SmartSteps

1. Think of a time where you worked out that another person wasn't really listening to you. How did you feel?

2. Think of a time where you got caught out for not really listening. What happened? What went wrong?

Chapter 37

The art of re-listening: Step 1 – Reflect

Imagine learning a skill that could save your marriage, gain new friends, make you a great parent AND help you lead both staff and customers!

"You never listen to me!"

How those words would hit me when my wife was annoyed with me!

"But I am listening!"

"No - you're not!"

Well, it was clear to ME that I was listening! My wife was talking; I was within earshot; both my ears were open - therefore I must be listening!

Of all the skills I have ever learned in my life, this is the most crucial one. **If I want other people to listen to me, I need to learn how to listen to them!**

This did not come naturally to me. I had to learn it. At first it felt awkward but now it is second nature. When you let a person know that you have really listened to what they have said, you will see amazing results:

- People will open up to you and really tell you what is on their heart.
- People will be attracted to you and more readily accept your advice.
- People will acknowledge your leadership and more willingly follow you.
- You will achieve far more than you ever could by yourself.

Let's check out a three-step procedure which you can use in **every** situation in your life.

Step 1 - Reflect

This is the first step that you can always do whenever anyone says anything to you involving any emotion. You simply reflect back to them what they have just said - in words that are similar to theirs.

> *"I can't stand that new manager that they've put in our section!"*
> *"Sounds like you're not getting on with him too well?"*

> *"I'm bored with this job!"*
> *"So you feel like there's nothing worthwhile to do?"*

a) Don't ...

- Don't use exactly the same words. *(otherwise you'll sound like the village idiot!)*
- Don't interpret the other person's statement or add your own material.
- Don't criticise what the person said.
- You don't have to agree (or disagree) with what the other person said.

b) Do ...

Simply accept what they said, and reflect it back to them, so they know that you have heard them. Play it back to them in your own words.

Start your reflections with words like:

- *"It sounds like ..."*
- *"You mean ..."*
- *"So you want to ..."*

What you're after is that the other person will respond with *"Yeah".* They will only say *"Yeah"* when they know that you've heard them and agree that you've got it right.

c) What if I get it wrong?

If you don't get an immediate *"Yeah"* from the other person, then have another go at it. Try saying to them:

"Sounds like I didn't hear you right. Tell me again."

Keep reflecting until you get the *"Yeah"* response from the other person.

What's the next step? It's in the next chapter, but DON'T READ IT until you have practiced this first step!

SmartSteps

1. The next time someone is speaking with you – and they're revealing things which include some emotion or feeling - practise this first step of re-listening.

   a) Feed back what they said to you – in words similar to (but not the same as) what they used

   b) Start your feedback with words like:

   - *"It sounds like ..."*
   - *"You mean ..."*
   - *"So you want to ..."*

   c) Keep doing this until you get the *"yeah"* response.

Chapter 38

The art of re-listening: Step 2 - Re-affirm

Before anyone will tell you how they really feel, they need to know that you accept them. How do you do that?

Have you ever noticed how people are sometimes reluctant to tell you what's really going on for them?

- An employee might be having a real difficulty at work - but they never let you know.
- A customer might be dissatisfied with your service - and the first you know of it is when they start going elsewhere.
- Your own partner - or your own children - simply don't tell you how they really feel.

Why not?

It's usually because **they're afraid that you won't approve of what they say.** They're worried that you might be critical of how they feel. They're concerned that if you really knew what they felt, that you might think less of them.

That's why Step 2 of "Re-Listening" really matters. You **re-affirm** the person as they share how they feel. But first - a quick recap!

Step 1 - Reflect

Your first response is to reflect back - in similar words - what you just heard them say *(See Chapter 37).* You do this until you get the *"Yeah"* response.

Step 2 - Re-affirm

You let them know that it's okay to feel that way.

> *"That's probably pretty important to you ..."*
>
> *"Boy - that must be hard for you ..."*
>
> *"If that were happening to me, I think I might feel the same way ..."*

This is not the same thing as agreeing with them! In fact, you might strongly disagree! Or you might feel that their issue is really trivial. Reaffirming them is not the same as agreeing with them or supporting their position. It simply lets them know **that you understand they feel that way.**

Imagine that you and a friend go to a movie. At the end, you think it was a terrific movie. But your friend says to you: *"That was a terrible movie! What a waste of money!"* How do you respond?

Step 1: - Reflect

Even though you disagree with them, you hold back on giving your opinion and decide to stay with the other person's feeling:

> *"So you didn't like the movie at all?"*

Step 2: - Re-affirm

Once again, you hold back on your own feelings, and you re-affirm **that it's okay for the other person to feel that way**.

> *"Yes - I hate it when I spend good money watching a movie I don't like"*

At this point you are not agreeing with the other person; you're simply letting them know that it's okay to feel annoyed when they sit through a movie they didn't really like.

Notice that you are holding back from announcing your opinion, and you're staying with how the OTHER person feels. (There'll be plenty of time for your opinions later on!) But if you can practise these two vital steps, you will become a great listener - and a great leader!

Step 3 - Next chapter – but don't read it yet – practise steps one and two first!

SmartSteps

1. Think back to a time where you were talking with someone – and their first step was to criticise you or disagree with you. What happened? How did you feel? How did it turn out?

2. The next time someone talks to you – and expresses an opinion – **hold back on giving YOUR opinion until you have spent the time listening to THEIR opinion.** You will be amazed at the different response you receive!

3. In all your conversations, practise these first two steps:

    a) **Reflect** - feed back to them what you heard them say in words similar to what they used.

    b) **Re-affirm** – let them know that it's understandable that they have that feeling (even if you don't understand it or disagree with it).

Chapter 39

The art of re-listening: Step 3 – Request

Imagine helping people to achieve their potential! Imagine leading people so they want to follow! Learn how to listen, and you'll learn how to lead!

If you've been practising the first two steps of being a great listener *(See Chapters 37-38)*, then by now, you're really ready to fly! Let's complete the exercise by learning Step 3.

But first - a quick recap!

Step 1 - Reflect

You reflect back - in similar words - what you just heard the other person say.

Step 2 - Re-affirm

You let them know that it's okay to feel that way.

Step 3 - Request

You invite them to tell you more about it.

This is the opportunity to let the other person talk for a while. You've let them know that you've heard them *(Step 1)*, and you've let them know that it's okay to feel that way *(Step 2)*. So now that they know that you are on their side, they should feel ready to give you the details which can help you both to work towards a solution.

> *"Can you tell me a bit more about that?"*
>
> *"So what happened then?"*
>
> *"How did you feel when ..."*

a) Ask open-ended questions

Don't ask questions that can be answered *"Yes"* or *"No"*. *"Yes"* and *"No"* are conversation killers. Open-ended questions keep the conversation going.

Don't ask: *"Did you feel scared?"* (Requires a yes/no answer, and is suggesting what their feeling might be).

A better question: *"How did you feel?"* (Open-ended)

b) Move from the general to the particular

Ask the other person for specific examples.

If the other person says *"I always feel worried"* then ask: *"Can you give me an example?"* or *"When was the last time that happened?"*

Putting it all together

As the other person tells their story, as soon as they mention an emotion or a feeling, **go back to Steps 1 and 2.** If you can practise this "Re-listening" on everyone you meet - business, family, friends, everyone - you will become the best listener they know, and you will become the best leader you can be!

Many years ago, my wife and I had a foster-son in his mid teens. One day during the school holidays, as I was trying to work from my home office, he just hung around for a while. When I looked in his direction, he said to me: *"I'm bored!"*

I resisted saying all the normal parental lines:

"Why don't you call your friends?"

"Why don't you ride your bike"

"After all the things I bought you for Christmas, how could you possibly be bored?"

I simply "re-listened". I said:

> *"You mean, it feels like there's nothing to do"* (Step 1)
>
> *"Yeah"*
>
> *"That must be awful to feel that way"* (Step 2)

He then started crying, and shared with me how much he missed his mother and his sisters. What a special moment I would have missed if I had simply dismissed him at the beginning!

Practise your listening. Aim to be a champion listener. Follow these 3 steps, and you are well on your way to becoming a champion leader!

SmartSteps

1. The next time someone in your family – or one of your close friends – shares something with you, intentionally go through the three steps. It may feel awkward when you start, but to the other person it will be such a refreshment to have someone who is **really listening.**

2. The next time someone at work – or someone on the team you lead – shares something with you, intentionally go through the same three steps. Keep practicing it until it becomes second nature. You will be amazed at the results!

Chapter 40

Relationships that build leadership

How do you form relationships with your team that will have a lasting impact?

The way you relate to others is one of the keys to your leadership. How do you relate to your team, your staff or your customers? Or more importantly, how do they relate to you?

Check out these key factors that will give you genuine relationships with lasting impact.

1. Have reproducing relationships

"You teach what you know, but you reproduce what you are" [1]

If you're leading a team - and investing into other people's lives, then you need to be aware that those whom you lead will become **somewhat like you.** They will pick up your strengths - and your weaknesses - and imitate them - and exaggerate them. So the first check-point for any leader is - *"Am I living a life that is worth copying?"*

2. Have coaching relationships

The key that marks out a **leader** in their relationships, is that they are always "coaching" those on their team. Not just "teaching" them (transferring information), but intentionally passing on values and skills. The person who is a true leader is always developing others to increase their skills and take on more responsibility. The person who has no interest in leadership will merely do their job and not worry about developing or training anyone else.

1 John C. Maxwell "The 360-degree leader: "Developing your influence from anywhere in the organisation". (Thomas Nelson TN 2005) p.246

3. Have two-way relationships

If you get carried away with the "coaching" model, you can end up with a very lopsided relationship - where it's all "one-way traffic". That is - you, with superior knowledge and skills - are graciously passing on your expertise - to those who are inferior in all these areas! **That is never the way a true leader relates!** Every relationship is a two-way street. You both have something to learn from each other. Every excellent school-teacher will tell you that they always learn things from their students. Good parents will always be open to learning things from their children. Good leaders will do likewise!

4. Have accountable relationships

This is one issue you must get right if you want to be a leader of excellence. Both you - and the members of your team - are accountable to each other. Your team is accountable for working under your direction to achieve your team goals - and you - as their leader - are accountable to them for developing them, training them, and unleashing them on an unsuspecting world!

I visited a well-established and high-profile church in London. Their senior pastor is a man with a well-known world-wide profile. He had gathered the youth leaders from his church - he and his wife hosted them for lunch -and then he spent some time chatting with them. I was fascinated to watch, because in this large church, a senior pastor would not normally have much to do with ground-level youth leaders.

After going around and commending them for the great work they were doing - singling out individuals for specific praise, he asked this great leadership question:

"What could we do differently here at this church that would help you do your job better - and make it easier for you?"

Here was a leader with great relationships! A leader who could make himself vulnerable to his team.

Think about those whom you lead - are you game to ask them a similar question?

SmartSteps

1. Think through the way you relate to those on your team. Write down **one step** to help your relationship to become more:

    a) Reproducing

    b) Coaching

    c) Two-way

    d) Accountable

Teamwork Unlimited

SECTION 5

How to multiply your leadership by building your team

Chapter 41

The danger of "Rambo Leaders"

There's a real excitement to leading your team single-handed. But flying solo brings huge dangers!

1. The Rambo Excitement

Imagine any *Rambo* movie. It doesn't matter which one. They are all roughly the same. Same script; same dialogue, just different costumes *(and Rambo gets older in each one!).*

Picture this: American soldiers have been captured and are being held at a cruel and deadly POW camp hidden deep in the jungle. After months of searching, the top brass can't even find this POW camp, so they call off the search, and just list these poor prisoners as "Missing in Action".

But Rambo will have none of this! He takes off by himself and single-handedly locates that POW camp, invades it, and overpowers every guard with sheer determination and a knife clenched between his teeth. He releases every one of "our boys", carrying the wounded across his shoulder. He completes his victory by tossing his last hand grenade behind him, so as he escapes with every one of "our boys", the final shot shows his hand grenade falling into the ammo dump of the POW camp, resulting in a huge fireball, with every evil terrorist being blown sky high.

Lots of businesses and organisations run like this! They have a dynamic entrepreneur who will not accept the complacency of their competitors. They go out and single-handedly raid and rescue clients and customers from the evil opposition. And all by themselves they go where no person has dared to go - they approach the unapproachable, win the unwinnable, and achieve the unachievable.

2. The Rambo Dangers

We need entrepreneurs in leadership! We need people who are prepared to break out of the mould!

But here are the problems with Rambo leadership:

a) The organisation won't go far

The organisation will never reach its potential - it will always be limited to what one human being can achieve.

b) The organisation won't continue

The organisation will never continue - as soon as the entrepreneur pulls back for any reason - the whole thing will collapse.

c) The leader will be crushed

As the enterprise grows - the work will get harder and harder - and the Rambo leader will have less and less satisfaction (and less fun!). Eventually they will run out of steam!

3. Team-work

Work solo - and you'll go fast.
Work in a team - and you'll go far.

If you want to make a lasting impact, grow your business to its potential and **enjoy** the fruit of all your hard labour, then at some stage you need to work with a team. That's where leadership comes in!

4. Raising other leaders

You're not a leader because you can attract **followers** to join up with you. You're a leader when you can attract and raise up **other leaders** to join up with you. The challenge for any leader is to create a culture where leadership will rise to the surface.

So - how do you build a leadership culture - where **everyone** achieves their full potential? – Next chapter!

SmartSteps

1. Think of an area of your leadership where you might be *going solo*.

    a) What are the advantages of this?

    b) What might be the limitations of this?

    c) What's the first step you can take to involve others in joining with you?

Chapter 42

How to build your team - with care

If you're focused on your business goals, you might lose sight of the people who matter. Here's how to build your team!

When I started out on my career path, I was very *gung-ho* about the whole thing. I was focused; I was driven; I was making plans; I was achieving goals. All very commendable!

But I had left something out of the equation - people! Sure - there were lots of people around me. There were colleagues on my team. I had customers and clients. I had bosses and work-mates. There were people everywhere!

But I didn't really value them. I didn't really appreciate them. Sure - I **needed** them - because they helped me achieve my goals. I needed them - because they had skills I didn't have. But I valued them **because of what they could produce for me.** I did not value them or care for them as people in their own right.

They felt taken for granted. They felt ignored. They saw me as cold and unfriendly. This was meant to be a team, but in reality it was a collection of individuals who were obliged to work together. I had no loyalty to them - and they had no loyalty to me.

Sound familiar? I keep finding this style of leadership around the planet. But you know - if you've ever been treated like that - you know how discouraging it can be.

"Nobody cares how much you know
Until they know how much you care." [1]

When you build a **real** team, you start by building with **care.**

1. People are more valuable than the work they produce

People really matter. They don't just matter because they can produce results for you. They matter because they are fellow human beings. We are all connected to each other as citizens of the one planet. We all have an intrinsic worth. The world champion athlete who is then severely injured in a car crash still has as much value as a person - even though they can no longer compete at the world level.

Of course some people will be absolutely strategic to us because of what they can accomplish for us. **But if you want people to achieve their best for you - then they need to know that you care about them.**

2. True caring is a result of true giving

The way you know that someone cares about you is that they **give** to you, rather than **taking** from you. If someone appears to be very friendly to you, but you know it's only because they want you to buy their product, then you will see through that insincerity straight away.

People will never follow someone who takes. But they will love to follow someone who gives. A true leader is a true giver.

a) Give of your talents

Whatever experience and abilities you have - share it with others. Invest into the members of your team so that your talents can help them reach their potential.

---

1 Theodore Roosevelt.

b) Give of your treasure

If you are generous to your team with your money and possessions, then that same giving spirit will spread like wildfire. By being generous to others, we communicate to them that **they** matter more to us than our **money** does.

c) Give of your time

This is the scarcest commodity in our fast-paced world. When you invest quality time into another person, you let them know that at **that** moment - they matter more to you than anyone else!

SmartSteps

1. Think of the people you relate to on your team. Write down one specific way that you can show genuine care to them by sharing with them ...

   a) Your talents

   b) Your treasure

   c) Your time

Chapter 43

How to build your team - with words

You have the power to build people up or to push them down. And this power comes from the strangest of places!

Imagine the joy of having the ability to inspire a person to their highest potential! But imagine the danger of having the capacity to dishearten a person and crush their hopes and desires! And yet every human being has this power. It resides within your tongue. You have the power of **words!**

1. Words are very powerful

"Sticks and stones may break my bones,
But names can never hurt me"

You know that's not true. I guarantee that at some stage in your life you have been hurt by something that someone has said to you. The very fact that children quickly learn that rhyme is because hurtful words **do** hurt. Words are a potent force available to us any time of the day. The wise leader will use words that build people up.

2. Words have the power of life and death

"The tongue has the power of life and death" [1] ***(NIV)***
- The Proverbs of Solomon

Everything you say will either lift people up or push them down. Everything you say will either draw people closer to you, or push them further away. Everything!

What you say might be very funny, or sarcastic, or witty. But it still has the power to inspire others to greatness or discourage them from even trying. If you want to build a leadership team, then you will use genuine words to inspire people to genuine greatness.

1 Proverbs 18:21

3. Encouragement really matters

Most of us put on a front so that we appear solid and untroubled to our work-mates. But below the surface, most of us need encouragement. So don't hold back! If you want to build a champion team, then learn to be a champion encourager.

4. Give private and public recognition

It's great to encourage others in private, but it adds extra weight when we praise them in front of others. At a youth group I'm involved with, at the end of the night we will often single out the leaders who put in the extra effort to run the night well. We will then publicly affirm them and bombard them with praise. What a motivation!

5. Correct in private

Never correct people in front of others. Give them the honour of doing it privately. Here is the test - can you build a person up as you challenge their behaviour? This is a mark of true leadership.

6. Be genuine

Words that are not backed up by action are meaningless. Don't use mere words as flattery, but use genuine words from a genuine heart to produce genuine encouragement.

7. The most important words of leadership

The 5 most important words: *"You did a great job!"*

The 4 most important words: *"What do you think?"*

The 3 most important words: *"Could you please ...?"*

The 2 most important words: *"Thank you!"*

The 1 most important word: *"We"*

The least important word: *"I"*

Who can you go to now - to build up with words that will inspire them to greatness?

SmartSteps

1. Think of a time when someone else used words to put you down or belittle you. What happened? How did you feel?

2. Think of a time when someone else used **insincere flattery** on you. What happened? How did you feel?

3. In your family, or friends, or work colleagues ...

   a) Are you using words in a way that might put them down or limit their potential? What can you change?

   b) Write down a list of the key people you relate to, and then list **the first step** you can take with each one to invest words into them that will build and strengthen them.

Chapter 44

How to build your team - with training

If you do most of your tasks by yourself - without anyone learning from you - you limit what can be achieved!

It's easy to think of training as a "special event". A course that you have to attend. A conference that you have to go to. A piece of paper that says you passed an exam.

Sure - training is all these things. But it is so much more. Successful companies in the world have learned that if you want to get ahead of your competitors, **then you make training a part of your every-day life.**

There are two main models of training in our modern world. Both of them are valuable. But the more **powerful** method is often under-used!

1. The Classroom Model

We all know the classroom model. We all grew up with it. Schools and universities specialise in it. Any serious profession places great stock in it. Conferences are based around it.

Here is the principle behind classroom training: The teacher - who has more **knowledge** than the students, primarily imparts **information** to the students. The effectiveness of this process can then be tested by getting students to recall this information in a written exam.

There is nothing wrong with this model. But it is never meant to be used in isolation! There is another **very powerful** learning model which is often overlooked.

2. The Apprentice Model

We're all familiar with this. Here's the way you learn a trade: the student is placed alongside their teacher in a real-life work situation. The teacher, who has more **experience** than the student, primarily imparts **skills** to the student. The effectiveness of this process can then be tested by seeing whether the student can display the skills they have been taught. This is how tradespeople are trained; this is how musicians are developed; this is how any skill is learnt.

3. Getting the balance right

We tend to think that the *professions* use the classroom model, and the *trades* use the apprentice model. No! **Both** matter in **all** situations. How does a surgeon learn to do a life-saving operation on a patient? Sure - there's a lot of classroom training that goes in, but they primarily learn **how** to do it by working alongside an experienced surgeon in an actual operating theatre!

Most of us learn best by the apprentice model. When I left school, I worked in a department store. How did I learn to sell lawn-mowers? By watching the experienced salesmen sell lawn-mowers!

How did you learn to drive? Sure - there was some study involved, but most of what you learnt was by having an experienced driver sit alongside you.

Here's the good news! The apprentice model is available to you every day in every situation! If you are doing a task by yourself - and there is no-one alongside you learning from you, then you are wasting a great training moment.

Companies that prosper are companies that train. Not just by sending people to conferences and courses. But by weaving a day by day training element into every facet of the workforce.

So – start building your team by training them!

SmartSteps

1. Which "more-experienced" person can you get alongside to ensure that **you** keep growing?

2. What "less-experienced" person can you have at your side to ensure that **everyone** keeps growing?

Chapter 45

How to build your team - with expectation

How do you keep the standards high - and inspire your team to achieve them?

To inspire and build a team, you need to have high, but realistic expectations. Set the expectations too low and no-one is inspired to achieve anything. Set the expectations too high and people will give up trying to reach the unreachable.

How do you motivate a team to achieve extraordinary results?

1. "We're going to do this well!"

Aim to do all things - even the little things - with a standard of excellence. If there's a meeting, are people there on time? Do they bring with them their pens, their diaries and their notebooks? If they're meant to have prepared something, do they normally do it?

You will want to model this with your own performance. If you keep shooting for excellence in all that you do, you will inspire your team to achieve the same.

And of course, you will also want to model this with grace, understanding and forgiveness. But you can still set the standard high!

2. It's okay to try something

The only way to inspire your team to reach far beyond themselves is to set a culture that it's okay to try something. That is, it's okay to try something out and then decide that maybe it wasn't the best way forward. Because if it's not okay to fail, then no-one will try anything!

3. Understanding success

Sometimes we think that success means *never failing.* If that's what your team members believe, they will never achieve anything!

Here's a better definition of success:
"I get knocked down - but I get up again" [1]

Failure means - I get knocked down one more time than I get up. Success means - I get up one more time than I get knocked down. If you can sow this value into your team, and model it with your own behaviour, you will develop and grow team members who have the courage to try new things and the strength to get up if they get knocked down the first time they try.

4. The best is yet to come

If you've been in business for a while, if you've achieved some good things together as a team, it's tempting to rest on your past glories. While it's certainly okay to celebrate every success and to remember them - you will achieve far more if you develop a culture that believes "the best is yet to come".

Everything that we take for granted now was once thought of as being impossible. If you can inspire your team with what seems impossible - and dream of what seems unreachable - who knows what dizzy heights you could hit!

"Most people don't fail because they aim too high and miss; Most people fail because they aim too low - and hit it"! - **Les Brown**

"Success is not the key to happiness. Happiness is the key to success. If you love what you are doing, you will be successful" - **Albert Schweitzer**

"Only those who dare to fail greatly can ever achieve greatly"
- Robert F. Kennedy

"Many of life's failures are people who did not realise how close they were to success when they gave up" - **Thomas A. Edison.**

1 Chumbawamba "Tubthumping". Released by Universal 1997

SmartSteps

1. Think of a time when one of your ideas didn't work out too well. What did you do to "get up again?"

2. Now think of a time when someone on your team failed at something.:

    a) How did **they** handle it?

    b) How did **others** handle it?

    c) How did **you** handle it?

    d) If something like this happens again, what is one thing you could do differently?

Chapter 46

How to build your team - by developing trust

How do you show your team that you're on their side? How do you gain their trust so you can move forward together?

One day my boss asked for my help. *"We're entertaining some corporate guests - and we'd like to take them out to dinner. Can you organise something for us all?"* No problems! I contacted our corporate guests - I found out what food they liked - and I tracked down a restaurant that would suit them well.

The place I had chosen was in a precinct that housed many restaurants. As we were walking there with all our guests, my boss noticed an Indian restaurant nearby. *"Hey - here's a great place to eat! Why don't we eat here?"*

Everyone obliged. After all - he was the boss! But I kept thinking to myself *"Why did I go to all the trouble to arrange something, to have my boss 'take over' at the last minute?"*

If your leadership style depends on your **controlling** everything - then you may well achieve your business goals but you might just crush your team along the way. There is another way! It's a little bit scarier and it sometimes takes a little bit longer. But it will build a committed team who will help you achieve spectacular results in the long term.

Here's how to motivate your team by trusting them, motivating them, empowering them and unleashing them.

1. Invest in your team

Keep investing into the lives of your team members. Affirm them, encourage them, correct them, train them.

2. Support your team

Let them know that you are cheering for them. Let them know that you will stand by them - no matter what. And back up your words with real actions!

3. Establish accountability

When your team members start to experience the high support that you are giving them, they will be more willing to accept the accountability that goes with it. They need to know that you are accountable to them for leading them well, and that they are accountable to you for achieving your agreed outcomes.

4. Incorporate their ideas

If you have an idea for achieving something, and one of your team members has another idea which is **almost** as good as yours, what do you do? If it will still help you to achieve your targets, then go with your team-member's idea. Even if it's **not quite as good as yours,** their ownership of their own idea will probably achieve far more in the long run.

5. Trust your team

Let them know that you trust them. You even trust them to take some risky decisions. You even trust them when **their** way isn't exactly the same as **your** way. **As long as you are achieving the agreed outcomes!**

6. Promote your team

As people on your team show they can be trusted - as they start to achieve great outcomes - demonstrate your trust by promoting them on your team. Give them larger areas of responsibility and larger rewards!

7. Celebrate with your team

Each time your team achieves significant goals, celebrate together! Have a few quiet drinks at the office. Present an award. Take them out for a meal. Surprise them with something outrageous. Make your team a place where they **love** to belong!

SmartSteps

1. Think of a time when you weren't trusted. What happened? How did you feel?

2. Now think through some opportunities you have to build trust in your team.

   a) What's one change that **you** can make that will help your team to trust you more?

   b) What's one area where you can unleash a team member by demonstrating trust in them?

Chapter 47

How to care for your customers by empowering your team

Leaders sometimes achieve their goals by controlling everything and everyone. But what happens when you empower your people and unleash them?

I was checking-in to my hotel room. The room I was shown was **way** below standard. The window was minimal, the bed was soft, the ensuite was cramped - indeed you would need to be somewhat of a contortionist to actually sit on the toilet with any degree of comfort! This wasn't what I'd paid for. I asked to be moved to another room.

"I'll have to check with the manager", I was told by the desk clerk. I waited. And waited. *"Sorry, the manager's out at the moment. I'll try and get him later in the evening!"* "Later in the evening" didn't cut it with me. I was tired from my day's journey. I wanted to lie down **right there and then.** I didn't want to do that in a room that was so woefully inadequate.

What did I learn about the leadership of that hotel? **That the staff had not been empowered to make their own decisions!** Everything had to be referred 'to the manager' - who was then able to stay in control of every facet of the business.

There were two down-sides to this style of leadership: **an employee who felt helpless, and a customer who felt dissatisfied!**

Some leaders achieve their goals by controlling everything and everyone. But here's why **empowering your team** is a much better option!

1. It develops your team

As you empower your team members, and allow them to make decisions, you grow them in a number of ways:

a) They learn to make good decisions.

By slowly allowing them to make decisions of increasing importance, you teach them how to make **good** decisions.

b) There is the opportunity to correct.

When they make mistakes (which they surely will!) there is the opportunity to turn this into a teachable moment. *(See Chapter 30).*

c) They learn to deal with the consequences.

Whatever decision your team-member makes, they learn to take responsibility for the consequences. It is something they 'own'. It is something they must deal with.

d) They get to enjoy the success

When your team member makes a good decision which leads to a good outcome, they get to celebrate this success! Because they own the decision, they own the result.

2. It serves the customer

When a customer has an issue that they want resolved, they want it resolved **now!** Not later in the evening. Not sometime next week. You know yourself how frustrating it is when any issue **you** have drags on and on! If you want to achieve brilliant customer satisfaction - **empower your staff to look after your customers!**

3. It builds for the future

You don't just want to train your team to be good employees. You want to train them to be good **leaders.** By modelling this empowering process for them, you are raising them up to be great leaders in the future.

This is what I was told as a young man in my very first job at a large department store: *"If you want to be promoted one day, then you need to make sure that you have trained someone else to take over your existing job!"*

Good advice! Empower your team!

SmartSteps

1. What areas are there where you control the decisions and actions of your team? Jot down one idea to get you started in each one of these areas:

   a) What training can I organise to help my team members deal with this?

   b) What systems can I put in place to support my team members in making this decision?

   c) What can I do to back my team members **even when they get it wrong?**

Chapter 48

The leadership of "Wow!"

How do you win and retain great customers? How do you ensure the loyalty of great staff? Never under-estimate the influence of "Wow!"

We've all experienced the "Wow" factor. When it happens to us, we know how powerful it can be!

I was flying with my long-haired young-adult son from Sydney to Melbourne. We were going down to watch a football match. I had left it to the last minute, and the only frequent flyer seats I could find were in business class.

So there we were - colourful and energised - sitting amongst the dull and dour suits of corporate-world. I guess we were fairly "inexpensive" business passengers - while the corporate types around us were relishing the free alcohol, my son and I contented ourselves with a single fruit juice each.

I imagine we stood out, as we soon attracted the attention of our dedicated Business Class Cabin Attendant. She came and looked after us. Chatted with us. Made us feel great about the flight we were taking. Showed her delight that I would spend time with my son.

Near the end of the trip, she brought out a new bottle of wine. It was a reasonably classy bottle - at the better and pricier end of the spectrum. *"I'd like you take this bottle with you - as our gift from Qantas to you."*

Wow! Imagine that happening! She engendered in us a feeling that **we wanted to fly with this airline again!** Every one of us probably has our "Wow!" story to tell. When something like this happens - **you talk about it!**

What can you do to create the "Wow!" factor in your business?

1. "Wow" your customers

"Wow!" is when you provide a service **far above the expectation of your customer.** What would it take to produce the "wow" factor in those whom you serve?

A colleague of mine was checking into a hotel and the receptionist offered him a hot, moist towel to refresh himself after his day's journey. "Wow!"

I was talking with a technician when I took my computer into the store for repairs. He needed to work on it for a few days - and as I had indicated that I lived some distance from the store, he said to me: *"I can drop it back at your house on my way home from work!"* Wow!

What can you do to **far exceed** your customers' expectations? What is your "bottle of wine", or "hot towel", or "home delivery"? Because if you can create the "wow" experience for your customers, two things will happen:

- They will want to keep doing business with you.
- They will tell all their friends.

2. "Wow" your staff

My business colleagues tell me that it takes more effort to find and retain great **staff** than to find and retain great **customers**. What can you do to create the "wow" effect with your staff? How can you **far exceed** their expectations?

It was our weekly staff meeting. After everyone arrived, the boss said *"No work today! I'm taking you all out to lunch!"*. A colleague of mine who works with a young staff team did the same thing - except he took them out to the Laserdome where they fired electronic guns at each other all afternoon!

What will happen when you overwhelm your staff with the "Wow" factor?

- They will want to keep working on your team.
- They will tell all their friends.

Wow! Now **that's** worth achieving!

SmartSteps

1. Think of the clients or customers whom you serve. What's one thing you could do to add the "Wow" factor into your relationship?

2, Think of the team that you lead. What's one thing you could do to add the "Wow" factor into your team?

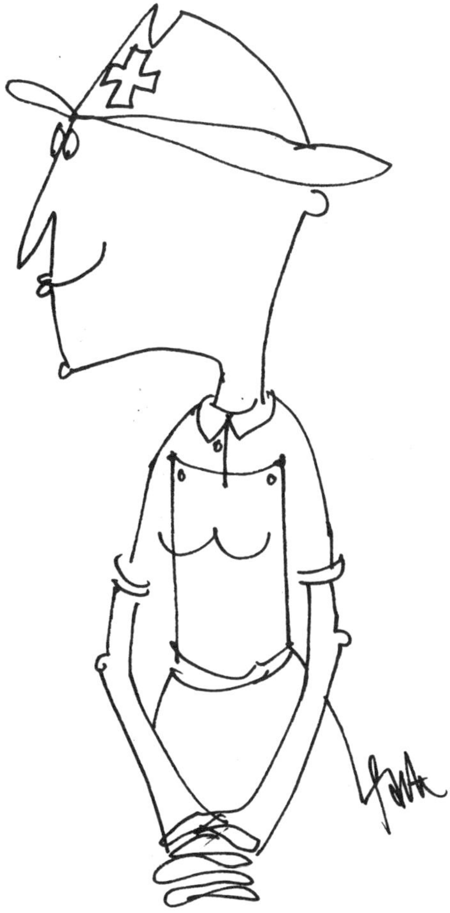

Chapter 49

Upside-down leadership - leading by serving

'A great leader needs to be a great servant.' A contradiction? Some of the greatest leaders of history have led this way - and changed the world!

What's your idea of a boss? What's your idea of a leader? Our traditional understanding of bosses and leaders is that they have all the power. They rule by the might of their status. They have the corporate perks, the reserved car spaces and the key to the executive washroom.

But if leadership is about **influencing** people - if leadership is about **making a difference** - then maybe we need to turn the whole idea of leadership on its head.

1. The real influencers in our society

Who are the heroes of our culture? We normally look to the rich and famous - business leaders, heads of government, sports stars and rock stars. But are they the true leaders of our world? Are they the ones whom people really respect?

There is another group of people in our world - extremely valuable, but sometimes hardly noticed. Usually overworked and underpaid. True servants. People like nurses, fire-fighters, teachers and para-medics. Community workers. Junior sporting coaches. Charity volunteers. Pastors and priests. Selfless individuals who quietly go about making a huge difference to our world.

Is it possible that these 'servants' have discovered the secret of true leadership?

2. Service wins customers

The idea of being a "servant" seems foreign to many of us. Something from a bygone era. Something for the lower classes. **But we all understand the importance of 'service' to a customer!**

What do people really want from a business? Whether it's your local fruit shop, a telco, a motor mechanic, or whatever ... what is the absolute key to winning customers back time and time again? Yes, price matters. So does quality. But in the end your customers will return when you give them **service** that outweighs your competitors.

3. Servant-leadership wins followers

A true leader is one who learns to be a true servant. If you want people to follow you - if you want people to support you - if you want to be an effective influencer of others - then they need to know that you have a heart to serve them. Have you ever had someone in leadership over you who was **not** interested in your welfare? Then you also know how reluctant you were to follow them!

How will people learn to trust you? How will people learn to listen to you? How will others commit themselves to supporting you through thick and thin? **If you want to be a great leader, learn first how to be a great servant.**

"The value of a man resides in what he gives and not in what he is capable of receiving." ***- Albert Einstein***

"Ask not what your country can do for you; ask what you can do for your country." ***- John F Kennedy***

"I came not to be served, but to serve, and to give my life as a ransom for many."[1] ***(NIV) - Jesus of Nazareth***

1 Mark 10:45

SmartSteps

1. Think of a time when someone provided outstanding service to you – which won you over to doing business with them or joining up with them. What happened? How did you feel?

2. Think of those whom you lead on your team. Write down one thing that you can do which will genuinely serve them. Are you game to do it? That is great leadership!

Chapter 50

Leadership to die for

How do you spot the difference between a genuine leader - and someone who's just "doing their job"?

1. The genuine shepherd

There is an ancient story about two men - each looking after a different flock of sheep. The first man was a shepherd. That's all he had ever been. He didn't own much in the world - all he had was his small flock. He owned his sheep and he knew them by name. He cared for his sheep because they were his livelihood.

The second man was just a hired hand. He was simply employed to do his job. He minded someone else's sheep. He kept watch over them - made sure they got fed - he did his job well. He clocked on at the beginning of his shift and then clocked off again.

At a distance, you couldn't tell the difference between the two. They both looked after their sheep. They both did their jobs well.

One night, a wolf came down to attack the sheep. The hired hand hadn't counted on this! When he realised that this wolf meant business, he ran as fast as he could to get himself away from any potential threat! After all - he wasn't being paid danger money! He got himself as far away from danger as possible, and left the sheep to fend for themselves.

The genuine shepherd, on the other hand, cared deeply for his sheep. He herded his flock to safety - he took on the wolf - he fought off the attack - even risking his own life to do so. The sheep were safe - because they had a shepherd who **genuinely cared.**

2. The genuine leader

How do you spot the difference between a genuine leader and someone who's just "doing their job"? A lot of the time they look exactly the same. Often you can only spot the difference **when things go wrong.** When the pressure is on - when it comes to the crunch - when there's dangerous territory - the hired hand will always act to protect their own skin; the genuine leader will act to protect those whom they lead. And yes - the genuine leader **will put their life on the line** for their team members.

Really?

Yes! The pages of history honour the valiant military leaders who have led their troops into enemy fire and paid the ultimate price themselves. Many will remember the brave captains of the New York Fire Department who led their troops into the blazing mess of the Twin Towers. There are countless stories of sporting captains who have continued to lead their teams to victory - even after they themselves have suffered injuries, and played on to finish the match with broken bones.

We would all hope that we never have to die to protect those whom we lead. But here is the question to ponder: **Would you be prepared to do it?** Your answer to that question will help you work out whether you are a genuine leader, or whether you're just "doing your job".

> *"We make a living by what we get, but we make a life by what we give."*
>
> ***- Winston Churchill***

> *"The hired hand is not the shepherd who owns the sheep ...*
> *The man runs away because he is a hired hand and cares nothing for the sheep. I am the good shepherd ... and I lay down my life for the sheep."*[1] *(NIV)*
>
> ***- Jesus of Nazareth***

1 John 10:12-14

SmartSteps

1. Putting your life on the line to protect someone whom you lead is an extreme situation. And yet is the marker that separates a genuine leader from someone who's just "doing a job". Write down the names of the key people on your team at the moment. Then work out something that you can do for each one to show them that you genuinely care for them.

2. Now go and do it!